MARSHALL MINI

SNAKES
AND OTHER REPTILES

D1313220

A Marshall Edition
Conceived, edited and designed by
Marshall Editions Ltd
The Orangery
161 New Bond Street
London W1S 2UF

First published in the UK in 2001 by
Marshall Publishing Ltd

10 9 8 7 6 5 4 3 2 1

ISBN 1 84028 391 2

Originated in Singapore by Master Image
Printed in Hong Kong by Imago

Consultant: Dr Richard Griffiths
Designer: Sarah Crouch
Managing Designer: Siân Williams
Design Assistant: Ella Butler
Art Director: Simon Webb
Managing Editor: Claire Sipi
Editorial Manager: Kate Phelps
Publishing Director: Linda Cole
Proofreader: Lindsay McTeague
Production: Nikki Ingram, Anna Pauletti
Picture Researcher: Su Alexander

MARSHALL MINI

SNAKES
AND OTHER REPTILES

Steve Setford

MARSHALL PUBLISHING • LONDON

Contents

The world of reptiles 6

Reptile groups 20

Life of reptiles 30

Guide to reptiles 52

Glossary 112

Index 116

Zoos and web sites 120

Acknowledgements 120

• •

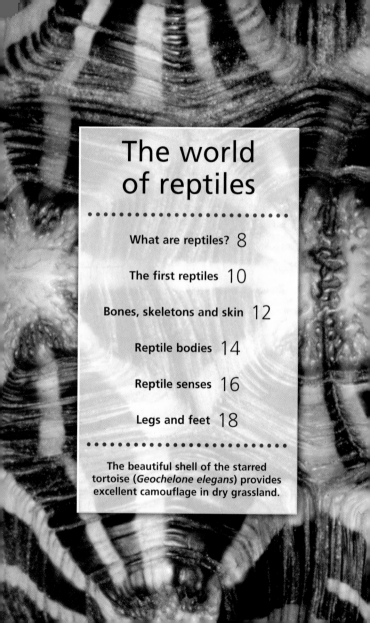

The world of reptiles

What are reptiles? 8

The first reptiles 10

Bones, skeletons and skin 12

Reptile bodies 14

Reptile senses 16

Legs and feet 18

The beautiful shell of the starred tortoise (*Geochelone elegans*) provides excellent camouflage in dry grassland.

What are reptiles?

There are over 6,500 different species of reptiles. Most of these scaly skinned, cold-blooded animals live on land, but turtles and some snakes live in water, while crocodiles are adapted to inhabit both.

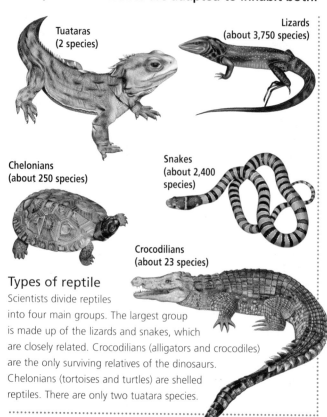

Tuataras
(2 species)

Lizards
(about 3,750 species)

Chelonians
(about 250 species)

Snakes
(about 2,400 species)

Crocodilians
(about 23 species)

Types of reptile

Scientists divide reptiles into four main groups. The largest group is made up of the lizards and snakes, which are closely related. Crocodilians (alligators and crocodiles) are the only surviving relatives of the dinosaurs. Chelonians (tortoises and turtles) are shelled reptiles. There are only two tuatara species.

8

Egg-laying reptiles

Most reptiles lay tough-shelled eggs after mating. The young develop inside the eggs and emerge fully formed, like small versions of the adults. Some reptile species give birth to live young. There are a few lizard species in which the female can give birth without mating first.

Female crocodile laying eggs in a nesting pit

Worm lizards prefer moist soil; they dehydrate and die quickly if it is too dry.

Worm lizards

There are about 150 species of worm lizards. These burrowing reptiles are like a cross between a lizard and a snake. They move forwards or backwards through their tunnels with ease as they search for food such as insects and worms.

Reptiles in folklore

Medusa

Folklore is full of stories of monster reptiles. The "hair" of Medusa in Greek mythology was a mass of snakes. All who gazed at her immediately turned to stone. Perhaps the most famous mythical reptile is the dragon. Although it is an evil creature in Western myths, in Chinese folklore it is gentle and a symbol of fertility and rebirth.

9

The first reptiles

Reptiles first appeared on Earth about 340 million years ago. They evolved from amphibians and soon became the most dominant animal group, ruling land, sea and air for more than 165 million years.

Dinosaurs

The most successful reptiles ever were the dinosaurs, which lived from 230 to 65 million years ago. Many were plant eaters. Others were fierce carnivores, such as *Tyrannosaurus*, which could be up to 15 m (50 ft) long, 5 m (16½ ft) tall and weigh up to 7 tonnes (6¾ tons).

A fossilised *Echmatemys* turtle

Fossil record

Scientists know about the evolution of modern reptiles from fossils found in rocks. Fossils are the buried remains of animals and plants that are turned into rocks over millions of years by heat and pressure.

Tyrannosaurus

10

Amphibians

The ancestors of reptiles are amphibians, which evolved from fish 380 million years ago. Amphibians need to return to water to lay their eggs. The young develop in the water, going through a larval stage before becoming adults. Early reptiles were more successful than amphibians because their tough-shelled eggs enabled them to move away from water and colonise dry land. The waterproof eggs stopped the baby reptiles inside from drying out.

Oriental fire-bellied toad

Chelonians first

Chelonians were the first of the modern reptile groups to evolve. Snakes were the last. Small mammals appeared during the Cretaceous period.

Evolution of reptiles (Millions of years ago)					
Palaeozoic era		Mesozoic era		Caenozoic era	
Carboniferous period	Permian period	Triassic period	Jurassic period	Cretaceous period	Palaeocene period to the present day
350	270	225	190	141	70
		Turtles, tortoises and terrapins			
			Crocodilians		
			Lizards		
					Snakes

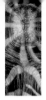

Bones, skeletons and skin

A reptile has an internal framework of bones called a skeleton, which supports and protects its body. Reptiles are vertebrates – they have a central spine made up of many small bones called vertebrae.

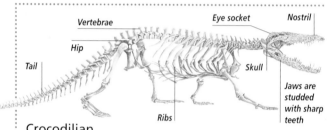

Vertebrae

Eye socket

Nostril

Hip

Tail

Skull

Jaws are studded with sharp teeth

Ribs

Crocodilian

A crocodilian has a long spine, a strong tail and four short legs. There are five toes on each front foot and four on each rear foot. The eye sockets and nostrils are high up on the thick skull.

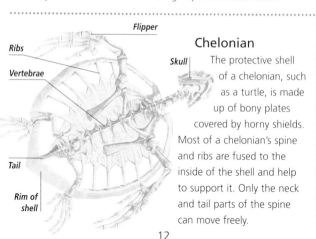

Flipper

Ribs

Skull

Vertebrae

Tail

Rim of shell

Chelonian

The protective shell of a chelonian, such as a turtle, is made up of bony plates covered by horny shields. Most of a chelonian's spine and ribs are fused to the inside of the shell and help to support it. Only the neck and tail parts of the spine can move freely.

Snake

A snake has a flexible spine containing up to 400 vertebrae. Except for the tail vertebrae, they all have a pair of ribs attached. The ribs are not joined at the bottom, so they can spread apart when the snake eats large prey. The jaws are only loosely joined so the mouth can open wide to swallow the snake's victims.

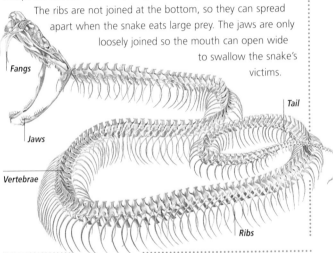

Fangs

Jaws

Vertebrae

Tail

Ribs

Scaly skin

A reptile has a scaly skin that acts as a waterproof covering to stop the reptile drying out. Like hooves and nails, the overlapping scales are made of a substance called keratin. Scales may be rough or smooth. Some reptile scales contain bony plates called osteoderms.

Small beadlike scales on a lizard

Crocodile scales reinforced by bone

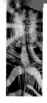

Reptile bodies

Beneath the scales, flesh and bones of a reptile are the organs that keep it alive. They include a heart for pumping blood, lungs for breathing and a digestive system for producing energy from food.

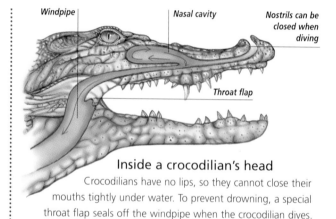

Windpipe

Nasal cavity

Nostrils can be closed when diving

Throat flap

Inside a crocodilian's head

Crocodilians have no lips, so they cannot close their mouths tightly under water. To prevent drowning, a special throat flap seals off the windpipe when the crocodilian dives.

The brain analyses information from the sensory organs and sends instructions to the body.

Skull protects brain

Brain

Lizard brain

The control centre of a reptile's body is its brain. The areas that deal with smell and taste are particularly well developed. Messages travel between the brain and the rest of the body via the spinal cord – a bundle of nerves running through the centre of the reptile's spine.

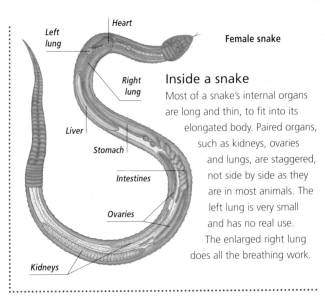

Left lung

Heart

Right lung

Liver

Stomach

Intestines

Ovaries

Kidneys

Female snake

Inside a snake

Most of a snake's internal organs are long and thin, to fit into its elongated body. Paired organs, such as kidneys, ovaries and lungs, are staggered, not side by side as they are in most animals. The left lung is very small and has no real use. The enlarged right lung does all the breathing work.

Inside a chelonian

The organs of a chelonian, such as a turtle, are squashed up to fit into its short broad body. Paired organs, such as the lungs, sit side by side. The intestines are coiled up, not stretched out as they are in a snake.

In reptiles, the sexual organs, bladder and digestive system connect to the cloaca, which leads to the anus.

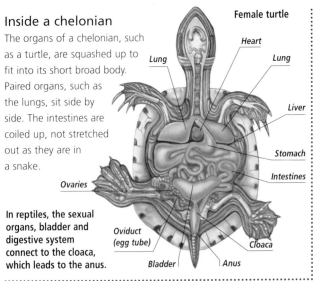

Female turtle

Heart

Lung

Lung

Liver

Stomach

Intestines

Ovaries

Oviduct (egg tube)

Cloaca

Bladder

Anus

Reptile senses

Like other vertebrates, reptiles use smell, sight and sound to understand the world around them. Some reptiles can also detect the body heat of distant prey or "taste" the prey's scent in the air.

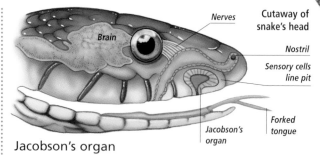

Nerves

Cutaway of snake's head

Brain

Nostril

Sensory cells line pit

Forked tongue

Jacobson's organ

Jacobson's organ

Lizards, snakes and chelonians smell through their nostrils, but they also have a Jacobson's organ – a pit in the roof of the mouth that "tastes" the air. A snake flicks its tongue in and out to pick up airborne scent molecules and transfer them to its Jacobson's organ. The pit of the organ is lined with special cells that analyse the scent.

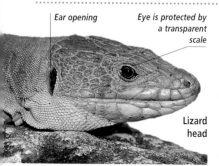

Ear opening

Eye is protected by a transparent scale

Lizard head

Sight and sound

Most reptiles can see well, but only crocodilians and lizards have external ear openings. Chelonians and snakes have poor hearing. Snakes "hear" by picking up vibrations in the ground with their skull bones.

Mysterious eye

Tuataras and many lizards have an eyelike structure beneath the skin on top of the skull. Sometimes called a third eye, it is the remains of a light-sensitive organ that may have been important to their reptile ancestors. Scientists once thought it was used to detect attacks from above. Today, it is thought to influence the amount of time the reptile spends basking in sunlight.

Tuatara head

Heat detectors

Pit viper snakes have heat-sensitive pits on either side of their head. The pits are lined with a layer of cells called thermoreceptors, which are linked to the brain by nerves. The thermoreceptors detect heat given out by the body of a prey animal. The messages they send to the snake's brain tell it not only the location of the prey but also how far away it is. The heat-pits allow the snake to strike with precision even in total darkness.

Heat-pit

Timber rattlesnake (a pit viper)

17

Legs and feet

Reptile legs and feet have evolved to suit different habitats. Some reptiles, such as snakes and a few lizards, have dispensed with limbs altogether.

Spur

Males have longer spurs than females and use them in courtship.

Vestigial limbs

On some snakes, such as boas and pythons, there are spurs at the base of the tail. These so-called vestigial limbs are the remains of legs – a reminder that snakes evolved from lizards millions of years ago. The spurs have no use in movement.

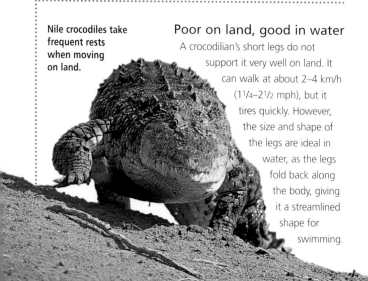

Nile crocodiles take frequent rests when moving on land.

Poor on land, good in water

A crocodilian's short legs do not support it very well on land. It can walk at about 2–4 km/h (1¼–2½ mph), but it tires quickly. However, the size and shape of the legs are ideal in water, as the legs fold back along the body, giving it a streamlined shape for swimming.

Expert climbers

Many lizards are good climbers. A few, including some geckos and skinks, can climb smooth surfaces such as glass and walk upside-down on ceilings. Even smooth-looking surfaces have microscopic bumps and pits on them. The lizards climb these surfaces using adhesive toe-pads. The pads are covered in tiny bristles that cling to the bumps and pits.

A gecko's toe-pads

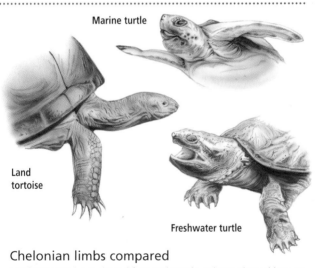

Marine turtle

Land tortoise

Freshwater turtle

Chelonian limbs compared

Land tortoises have clawed feet and sturdy, column-shaped legs to support their weight. Freshwater turtles have webbed, clawed feet that enable them to both move on land and swim in water. Marine turtles, which rarely come ashore, have clawless flippers, not legs.

Reptile groups

Lizards 22

Snakes 24

Chelonians 26

Crocodilians 28

A chameleon's remarkable swivelling eyes enable it to look behind, below and above, as well as straight ahead.

Burrowing tortoises

Some chelonians, such as
the gopher tortoise,
dig burrows which
they can escape into
if the temperature
or humidity outside
becomes intolerable.
The gopher tortoise
may share its burrow,
which can be up to 14 m (46 ft)
long, with other small animals.

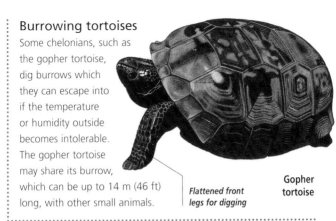

*Flattened front
legs for digging*

**Gopher
tortoise**

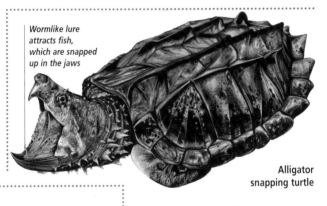

*Wormlike lure
attracts fish,
which are snapped
up in the jaws*

**Alligator
snapping turtle**

Freshwater turtles

Many chelonian species live in or near
fresh water. In cold weather, they may
burrow into the mud on the bottom
of a river, lake or pond to hibernate or
rest. They have webbed feet and many
are carnivorous. The alligator snapping
turtle lures prey with a pink fleshy flap
on its lower jaw that looks like a worm.

Crocodilians

These fierce predators live
in or near water in tropical
parts of the world. They lurk
in the water with just their eyes,
ears and nostrils showing, suddenly lunging
to attack prey drinking at the waterside.

Adapted for water

Crocodiles swim by
swishing their broad
muscular tails from side
to side, and paddling
and steering with their
webbed rear feet. They
can close their nostrils and
ears when they submerge. A
transparent third eyelid protects
the eyes when underwater.

Nile crocodile

Crocodilian movement

On muddy river banks, crocodilians slither along on their bellies; but
on dry land, they usually lift their bodies off the ground and walk. To
catch prey, some can make short gallops at up to 18 km/h (11 mph).

Belly slide: the
legs are splayed
out on either
side of the body.

Baby Nile crocodile hatching from its egg

Crocodilian heads

Crocodiles usually have narrower snouts than alligators and caimans. When crocodiles close their mouths, the fourth tooth on the lower jaw is visible. Gavials are easily identified by their long snouts with small, piercing teeth.

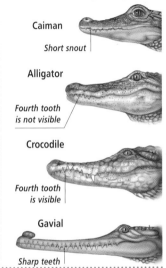

Caiman

Short snout

Alligator

Fourth tooth is not visible

Crocodile

Fourth tooth is visible

Gavial

Sharp teeth

Young crocodilians

When baby crocodilians are ready to hatch, they call out to their mother. She digs open the nest and may even crack the eggs with her jaws and pull the babies free. The young stay close to their mother after hatching, often resting on her back, where they are safe from predators.

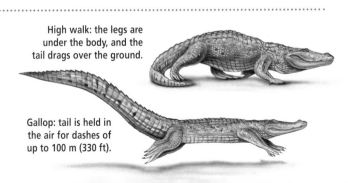

High walk: the legs are under the body, and the tail drags over the ground.

Gallop: tail is held in the air for dashes of up to 100 m (330 ft).

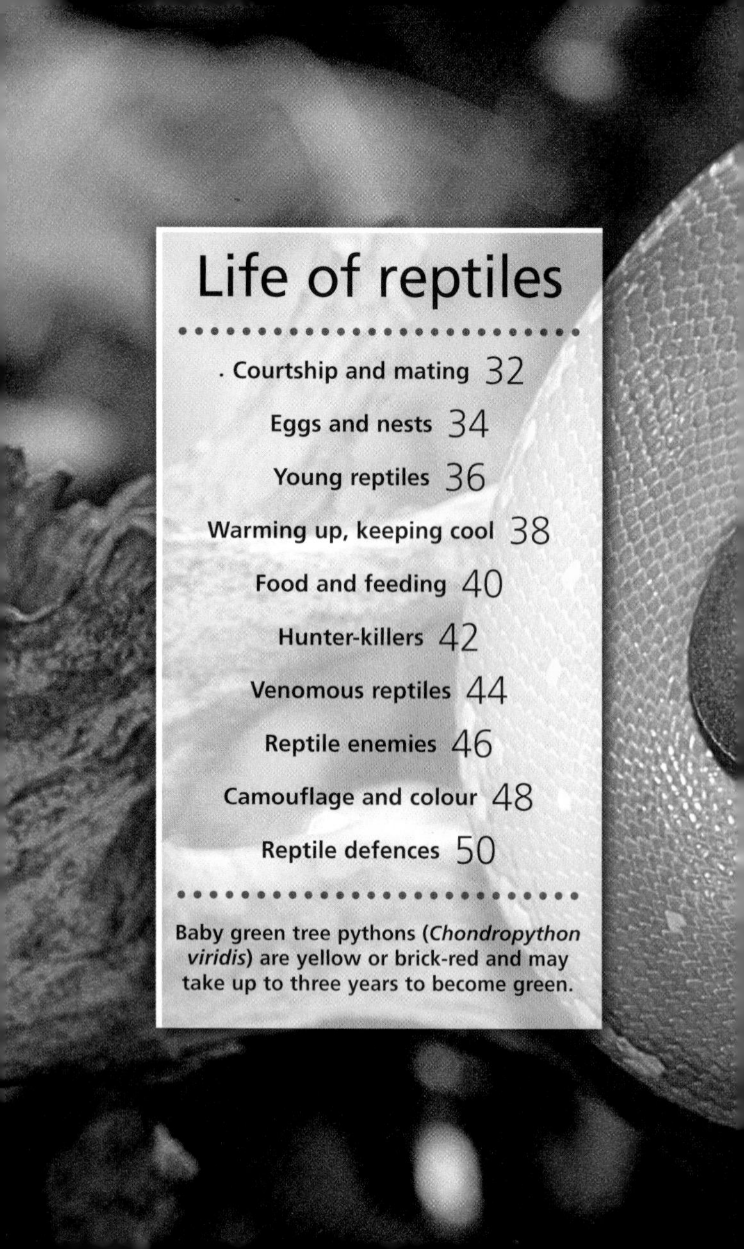

Life of reptiles

. Courtship and mating 32

Eggs and nests 34

Young reptiles 36

Warming up, keeping cool 38

Food and feeding 40

Hunter-killers 42

Venomous reptiles 44

Reptile enemies 46

Camouflage and colour 48

Reptile defences 50

Baby green tree pythons (*Chondropython viridis*) are yellow or brick-red and may take up to three years to become green.

Courtship and mating

Reptiles use a variety of signals, scents and displays to attract members of the opposite sex in order to reproduce. Males compete, sometimes violently, for the right to mate with females.

Male monitor lizards fighting

Fighting for dominance

At the start of the breeding season, male monitors take part in wrestling matches to assert their dominance over other males. Two males may rear up on their hind legs, using their tails to balance, and grapple with their forelegs until one is pushed over and defeated.

Special muscles extend the colourful fan

The male anole's display helps to solve disputes over territory or mates without resorting to fighting.

Taipans mating

Snake courtship

A female snake attracts a male mate using a special scent. Courtship involves the male rubbing his chin along her back and flicking his tongue over her body. The snakes intertwine their bodies so that the male can insert one of his two sex organs (hemipenes) into her cloaca for mating to take place.

Giant tortoises

A male giant tortoise will sniff a female to see if she is ready to mate. He then butts or rams her shell to show his interest in her. If the female accepts him, he must then clamber up on to her shell, so that the two tortoises are in the correct position for mating. During mating, which sometimes lasts for several hours, the male roars loudly now and again.

The larger male dwarfs the female.

Ritual display

To impress potential female mates, the male anole lizard performs a ritual display, bobbing his head up and down and extending the colourful fanlike flap of skin under his throat. As well as attracting females, it also serves to warn rival males to stay away.

Eggs and nests

After mating, most female reptiles lay eggs from which their young hatch. The eggs usually have soft flexible shells, but some are hard-shelled, like birds' eggs.

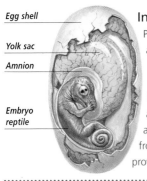

Egg shell

Yolk sac

Amnion

Embryo reptile

Inside an egg

Protected by the shell and cushioned from knocks by a bag of fluid called the amnion, the young reptile, or embryo, develops in safety inside the egg. The shell absorbs oxygen and water, which are vital for the embryo's growth, from the outside. The yolk sac provides the embryo with food.

Laying the eggs

A female turtle finds a safe place to dig a nesting burrow. She lays her eggs in the burrow, covers them over with soil, and then leaves the eggs to incubate and hatch on their own. The majority of reptiles behave in the same way, but crocodilians and a few snakes and lizards guard the eggs until they hatch.

Female turtle laying eggs in sand

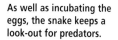

As well as incubating the eggs, the snake keeps a look-out for predators.

Incubating the eggs

The females of a few snake species do not bury their eggs and leave them to incubate, but coil their bodies around them instead. By contracting her body muscles, the mother generates enough heat to keep the eggs at just the right temperature.

Guarding the nest

The female Nile crocodile buries her eggs in a pit near water. She guards the nest while the eggs incubate, scaring off animals such as hyenas or monitor lizards that try to raid the nest.

The female does not leave the nest, even to feed, until her eggs hatch.

She will attack any intruder that comes too close

Young reptiles

Apart from crocodilians, most reptiles have no interest in their young once they hatch or are born. The young reptiles are miniature replicas of their parents and are able to feed themselves.

Devoted mother

A female crocodile is a devoted mother. When her babies hatch from their eggs, she carefully picks them up in her jaws and carries them to a quiet pool, where she guards them for some time.

Nile crocodile and babies

Babies are carried gently in mother's mouth

Journey to the sea

When young marine turtles hatch from their eggs, they dig their way out of the sand and race to the sea. Many are eaten by crabs and seabirds on the way, and still more by sharks and other fish lurking offshore. Fewer than 1 in 100 reach adulthood.

Time to hatch

Baby lizard hatching from egg

A baby reptile uses a sharp lump on the tip of its snout to cut its way out of its egg. This egg tooth falls off after the baby has hatched. In chelonians, crocodilians and some lizard species, the sex of the young depends on the temperature inside the nest. Lower temperatures produce more females, and higher ones more males.

Two-striped forest pit viper

Live young

In some species of lizards and snakes, such as the two-striped forest viper, the mother keeps her eggs inside her body until they hatch. She gives birth to live young, but still abandons them soon after birth.

By all hatching together, some turtles are sure to survive the attentions of predators.

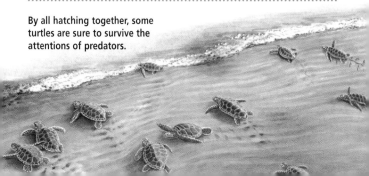

Warming up, keeping cool

A reptile is cold-blooded. This means that it cannot make its own body heat like a mammal or a bird can. Its temperature depends on the temperature of its surroundings.

Basking gives reptiles, such as this iguana, the warmth they need to be active.

Getting warm

When reptiles get cold, they grow sluggish and unable to find food or escape predators. After a cool night, many reptiles spend the early morning basking – lying in the sunshine to warm up their bodies. Once their bodies are the right temperature, they can hunt or forage for food.

Sandfish lizard

Desert life

In sandy deserts, there may be no shady spots to hide from the scorching heat. The sandfish lizard digs down into the sand to hide from the sun's rays. Some burrowing desert reptiles stay under the sand all day, emerging only after sunset to hunt in the cool of the night.

American alligator

Cooling down

When a crocodilian gets hot, it opens its jaws to let heat evaporate from the inside of its mouth. It may also take to the water to cool off. Some alligators shelter from the midday heat in riverside burrows.

Pet tortoise hibernating in straw

Winter sleep

In cooler climates, it may be too cold in winter for a reptile's body to function, so it may go into a sleeplike state called hibernation. Its heart rate and breathing slow down and its digestive system stops working. Some reptiles go into a similar state when food or water are scarce. They "wake up" when conditions are more favourable.

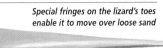

Special fringes on the lizard's toes enable it to move over loose sand

Lizard "swims" through sand with its legs as it look for beetles and millipedes under the surface

Streamlined body

Food and feeding

Like all animals, reptiles must eat to survive, but many reptiles eat far less often than mammals. An adult crocodilian can survive for months without feeding, staying alive by using up its own body fat.

Snail-eating snake

This snake eats only snails. It inserts its lower jaw into a snail's shell and twists it, sinking its teeth into the soft body and pulling it out. As it feeds, the snake breathes air stored in its lungs, because the struggling snail produces slime that clogs up the snake's nostrils.

Plant food

The marine iguana can dive for 20 minutes as it forages for seaweed on submerged rocks. While underwater, its heart rate and blood flow slow down to reduce heat loss and conserve oxygen. It feeds every 3 to 5 days.

Marine iguana feeding underwater

Chelonians do not have teeth. They use the sharp edges of their horny jaws to slice up their food into pieces that they can swallow easily.

Chelonian diets

Crocodiles and snakes are meat eaters, and so are most lizards, but chelonians have a more varied diet. Adult tortoises eat mainly plants – they are too slow-moving to be good predators. Freshwater turtles feed on worms, snails and other small animals. Some lie in wait to snatch faster-moving prey such as fish. Marine turtles eat crabs, jellyfish, molluscs, fish and even seagrass.

Changing tastes

Some reptiles eat different foods as they grow. Baby Nile crocodiles feed on insects, but then move on to fish, birds and crabs as juveniles. Fully grown adults prey mainly on mammals – often large ones, such as buffalo.

Baby Nile crocodile with insect

41

Hunter-killers

Many carnivorous reptiles are highly efficient predators, with a wide variety of techniques for stalking, capturing and devouring their prey.

Squeezing to death

As if hugging its prey to death, a constricting snake coils its body tightly around its victim. It squeezes harder and harder until the prey can no longer breathe and dies by suffocation. It may take more than an hour to swallow large animal prey, and weeks or even months to digest it.

Jaws inch their way along prey

African python

Prey is swallowed headfirst

One eye tracks prey, while the other watches out for danger

Chameleon

This sharpshooter can flick out its long tongue to scoop up insect prey in just six one-hundredths of a second. Prey is glued to the tongue by sticky mucus on the tip and then flicked back into the mouth. The tongue, which may be longer than the chameleon's entire body, is curled up inside the mouth when not in use.

Sucking food in

The freshwater Mata-mata turtle has an unusual way of catching fish. It lies still with its mouth wide open. When a fish swims past, it expands its throat suddenly and sucks the surprised fish straight into its mouth.

By expanding its throat, the turtle creates a strong current that pulls the fish towards it

Waterside terror

A Nile crocodile tackles prey as large as antelopes, zebras and wildebeest. It seizes prey with a sudden lunge, then drags it into the water and drowns it. It grips the flesh and twists it to tear off large pieces, which it swallows without chewing. Crocodiles sometimes share their meals.

A Nile crocodile hurls itself at a zebra drinking by the waterside.

43

Venomous reptiles

Some reptiles have developed the ability to kill prey and enemies by injecting them with a toxic chemical called venom. Of all the thousands of reptile species, only a few hundred are venomous, including about 50 whose bite is deadly to humans.

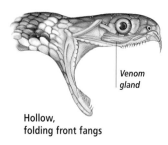

Venom gland

Hollow, folding front fangs

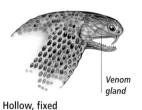

Venom gland

Hollow, fixed front fangs

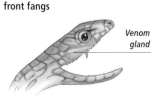

Venom gland

Grooved, fixed rear fangs

Fangs and venom

Snake venom is made in glands on each side of the upper jaw. It is injected into prey by long teeth called fangs. Rattlesnakes and vipers have hinged fangs at the front of the mouth that fold back when not in use. Cobras have fixed fangs at the front. In front-fanged snakes, venom is pumped through the fangs, which are hollow. Back-fanged snakes, such as boomslangs, have fixed fangs at the rear of the mouth. Venom drains down grooves along the edge of the fangs.

Rattling tail warns enemies that the snake is about to strike

Boomslangs hunt small animals such as chameleons, frogs and birds.

Highly toxic

One of Africa's most venomous snakes, the boomslang has been known to kill humans. Its highly toxic venom causes breathing difficulties and internal bleeding. Fortunately, it only bites when it is cornered.

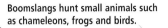
Gila monster

Poisonous lizards

The only venomous lizards are the gila monster and the Mexican beaded lizard. Both have venom glands in their lower jaws. Venom is not injected, but seeps into the wound when the lizard bites its victim.

Paralysing venom

The largest of all rattlesnakes, the eastern diamondback is the most dangerous snake in the USA. Its venom is not as toxic as that of many other snakes, but it injects a large amount into its victims, paralysing them quickly. The venom also starts to break down the tissues of the prey's body, making digestion easier.

As the mouth opens wide, the fangs swing forwards, ready to bite.

Eastern diamondback   45

Reptile enemies

Even large and poisonous reptiles have enemies. The Nile crocodile, for example, may be killed by predatory lions and angry hippos or elephants, and the venomous cobra by the swift, agile mongoose.

Small but effective

The cobra is a fearsome snake, but it meets its match in the mongoose. This small mammal is immune to its venom. It uses its speed to avoid the snake's lunges and sink its razor-sharp teeth into the back of the cobra's neck.

Indian mongoose

Giant threat

Nile crocodiles sometimes get killed when they try to prey on baby elephants. The mother elephant will fiercely defend her calf. She may even trample the attacker to death and hurl its body into a tree.

Elephants bathing

Human predators

For many reptiles, humans pose the greatest threat. Some reptiles are hunted for their meat or because people think they are dangerous. Others are captured and sold as pets, or are killed for their skins, which are used for leather goods. Many reptiles die when their habitats are destroyed by farming, tourism or building projects.

Woman with snake skin

Hunters from the sky

Snake eagles feed mostly on reptiles, particularly tree snakes. They drop down on their prey from a perch and snatch the snake with their feet. Their short strong toes have a rough surface that holds the wriggling catch in a vicelike grip. The secretary bird has a more unusual hunting technique – it tries to stamp snakes to death. If that does not work, it carries its prey high into the air and drops it on to rocky ground.

Crested serpent eagle with prey

Camouflage and colour

Many reptiles use their colour, shape and body pattern to blend in with their surroundings. This helps them to creep up unseen on their prey and to avoid being spotted by predators. Colours may also be used as warning signals to other animals.

Quick-change artists

By varying the mix of different pigments in their skin, chameleons can change their colour to merge with the background. Males also use bright colours to warn off rival males or to impress females. When males compete over territory, the victor displays bright colours. The loser grows darker and retreats.

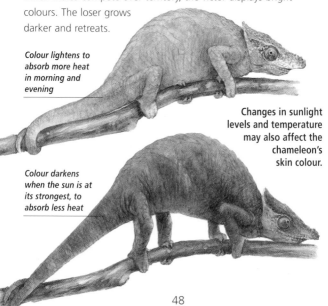

Colour lightens to absorb more heat in morning and evening

Changes in sunlight levels and temperature may also affect the chameleon's skin colour.

Colour darkens when the sun is at its strongest, to absorb less heat

The blue-tongued skink points its tongue at attackers.

Startling colour

Some reptiles, such as the blue-tongued skink, use colour to startle and frighten attackers. If cornered, this lizard opens its mouth wide, sticks out its bright blue tongue and hisses. This fools the predator into thinking that the lizard is more fearsome than it really is.

Warnings and mimicry

Some venomous snakes, such as coral snakes, use bright colours to warn predators to stay away. The harmless scarlet king snake copies the coral snake's colours so that predators think it, too, is venomous. This is called mimicry.

Scarlet king snake

Bright bands are almost identical to those on the coral snake

Blending in

Being stealthy hunters, it is not surprising that many snakes are masters of disguise. The green skin and long thin body of the tree-dwelling vine snake make it indistinguishable from the lush foliage high up in the canopy of the tropical rainforest.

Vine snake in foliage

49

Reptile defences

Some reptiles have special tricks or tactics to help them survive when they cannot escape or hide from predators. Many lizards, for example, can shed their tail to evade a predator's grip.

Playing dead

If hissing and puffing loudly do not deter a predator, the grass snake pretends to be dead by lying perfectly still, with its tongue hanging out of its mouth. Most predators will avoid a dead animal, as it may have died of a disease that could also infect the predator.

Grass snake playing dead

Chemical weapons

Although it looks vulnerable, the stinkpot turtle is quite capable of defending itself. Not only does it give a nasty bite but it also releases a chemical that is so foul-smelling that few enemies have the stomach to go near it.

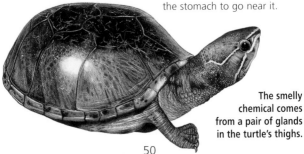

The smelly chemical comes from a pair of glands in the turtle's thighs.

Basilisk running over water

Walking on water

A basilisk escapes predators by dropping off its perch on a riverside tree or bush and running over the water's surface, supported by scaly fringes on its long toes. As it loses speed, it starts to sink, so it swims away underwater, coming up for air after a safe distance.

The art of bluffing

The frilled lizard does not flee from danger, but faces it head-on. When threatened, it opens its mouth wide and raises the frill around its neck. The frill may be up to four times the width of the lizard's body, making a predator think that it has taken on a much larger, more fearsome lizard. The frilled lizard adds to the menacing effect by bobbing its head, lashing its tail, hissing and waving its arms.

Frill is a large flap of skin around the neck

Guide to reptiles

Tuataras 54

Lizards 55

Worm lizards 76

Snakes 78

Chelonians 96

Crocodilians 108

An adult and a juvenile American alligator (*Alligator mississipiensis*) bask beside a rushing river.

Tuataras

Often referred to as living fossils, tuataras are the last survivors of a group of reptiles known as Rhynchocephalia (meaning "beak heads"), which roamed the Earth 60 million years ago.

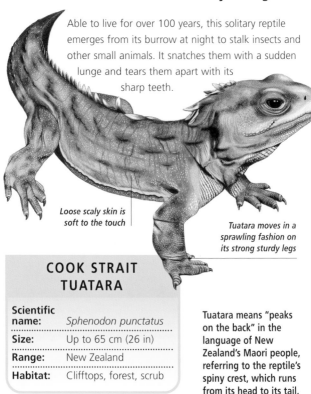

Able to live for over 100 years, this solitary reptile emerges from its burrow at night to stalk insects and other small animals. It snatches them with a sudden lunge and tears them apart with its sharp teeth.

Loose scaly skin is soft to the touch

Tuatara moves in a sprawling fashion on its strong sturdy legs

COOK STRAIT TUATARA

Scientific name:	*Sphenodon punctatus*
Size:	Up to 65 cm (26 in)
Range:	New Zealand
Habitat:	Clifftops, forest, scrub

Tuatara means "peaks on the back" in the language of New Zealand's Maori people, referring to the reptile's spiny crest, which runs from its head to its tail.

Lizards

Lizards are the largest reptile group. Most have four legs, but there are some legless species and others, such as skinks and snake lizards, that have extremely small limbs.

Crest of comblike spines

COMMON IGUANA

Scientific name:	*Iguana iguana*
Size:	1–2 m (3¼–6½ ft)
Range:	Central & South America
Habitat:	Forest, trees near water

This plant eater basks in riverside trees. When threatened, it hurls itself into the water and swims off. If cornered, it can defend itself fiercely with its teeth and claws.

To escape from danger, the chuckwalla hides in a narrow rock crevice and puffs up its body with air, making itself almost impossible to dislodge.

CHUCKWALLA

Scientific name:	*Sauromalus obesus*
Size:	28–42 cm (11–17 in)
Range:	SW USA, Mexico
Habitat:	Rocky desert

MARINE IGUANA

Scientific name:	*Amblyrhychus cristatus*
Size:	1.2–1.5 m (4–5 ft)
Range:	Galápagos Islands
Habitat:	Rocky coasts

Glands in the nasal cavity expel salt that the iguana takes in as it feeds at sea

The marine iguana is the only lizard that is truly at home in the sea, diving to depths of 9.3 m (30 ft) as it forages for seaweed. It spends most of its time basking on volcanic rocks on the shore.

Once warmed by the morning sun, this daytime hunter bounds over the rocks in search of insects and small lizards. It races away from predators on its strong hind legs.

"Collar" of light and dark neck bands

COLLARED LIZARD

Scientific name:	*Crotaphytus collaris*
Size:	20–35 cm (8–14 in)
Range:	SW USA, Mexico
Habitat:	Rocky hillsides, forest

Strong tail used to lash out at attackers

FOREST IGUANA

Scientific name:	*Polychrus gutterosus*
Size:	Up to 50 cm (20 in)
Range:	Tropical South America
Habitat:	Forest

Lizard can cling to a branch using its back legs alone

Colour helps to hide lizard on branch

This tree-dwelling lizard lies motionless on a branch, with its flattened body pressed against the surface, as it waits for insect prey to come within range.

Long tail powers the iguana through the water; partially webbed feet help steer

RHINOCEROS IGUANA

Scientific name:	*Cyclura cornuta*
Size:	Up to 1.2 m (4 ft)
Range:	West Indies
Habitat:	Dry scrubland

Hornlike scales on the male's snout give the lizard its name

Despite its large size, the rhinoceros iguana is very shy and quickly retreats into its burrow at the first hint of danger. It lives among thorn bushes and cacti, feeding on plants, worms and mice.

This lizard thrashes its spine-studded tail back and forth to defend itself against predators. It feeds by day on grass, fruit, leaves and flowers, sheltering in rock crevices at night.

Plump body and small turtlelike head

PRINCELY MASTIGURE

Scientific name:	*Uromastyx princeps*
Size:	23 cm (9 in)
Range:	E Africa
Habitat:	Rocky, stony land

Tail makes up more than half the lizard's total length

COMMON AGAMA

Scientific name:	*Agama agama*
Size:	Up to 20 cm (8 in)
Range:	W, C & E Africa
Habitat:	Rocky open savanna

Agamas live in groups of 2 to 25, ruled by one dominant male who defends the group and its territory. In the rainy season, the females lay four to six eggs in moist soil.

Agamas emerge at dawn to bask in the sunshine and feed on insects and spiders.

58

SOA-SOA WATER DRAGON

Scientific name:	*Hydrosaurus amboinensis*
Size:	1.1 m (3½ ft)
Range:	New Guinea, Indonesia
Habitat:	Rainforest

The soa-soa lives close to rivers. The male has a crest on his tail, which he raises to impress females and rival males. Despite its fierce, dragonlike appearance, the soa-soa feeds mainly on plants.

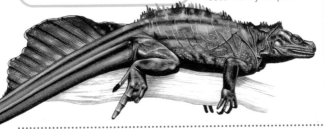

Tail is raised and repeatedly rolled and unrolled to warn off attackers

ARABIAN TOAD-HEADED AGAMA

Scientific name:	*Phrynocephalus nejdensis*
Size:	12 cm (5 in)
Range:	SW Asia
Habitat:	Desert, semi-desert

This burrowing lizard shuffles its body to and fro to bury itself rapidly in the sand. Its overhanging brow and thick, tightly closing lids keep sand out of its eyes. It gives birth to live young.

If alarmed, the lizard raises its body on its long legs

Green blends in with lichen-covered tree bark

Males use their horns in battles over females and territories

JACKSON'S CHAMELEON

Scientific name:	*Chamaeleo jacksonii*
Size:	11–12 cm (4–5 in)
Range:	E Africa
Habitat:	Savanna vegetation

The male has three large horns on his head. The horns help Jackson's chameleons to recognise each other and to tell the sexes apart.

When alarmed, this chameleon turns a darker shade and inflates its body with air. The female lays 20 to 30 eggs, which she buries in the ground.

EUROPEAN CHAMELEON

Scientific name:	*Chamaeleo chamaeleon*
Size:	25–28 cm (10–11 in)
Range:	SW Europe, N Africa
Habitat:	Bushes in dry country

Tail wraps around a branch to hold the chameleon steady as it watches for insect prey

This large chameleon feeds on small birds, as well as insects. To make itself less noticeable to predators and prey alike, it sits on a branch and gently rocks from side to side, like a leaf swaying in the breeze.

Body pattern and colour hide chameleon among leaves

MELLER'S CHAMELEON

Scientific name:	*Chamaeleo melleri*
Size:	54–58 cm (21–23 in)
Range:	E Africa
Habitat:	Savanna vegetation

FLAP-NECKED CHAMELEON

Scientific name:	*Chamaeleo dilepis*
Size:	25–36 cm (10–14 in)
Range:	Tropical & S Africa
Habitat:	Forest, scrubland

This chameleon has flaps of skin at the back of its head, which it raises as a threat to warn off rival chameleons. On tree bark it is yellow and reddish brown, but it turns green when among leaves.

Each eye can swivel independently

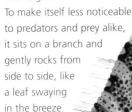

This lizard is thought to bring good luck to the homes it visits. It feeds mainly on insects, mice and small birds. The female lays two sticky eggs, which she "glues" to an upright surface.

The male's mating call of "tokeh" or "gecko" can be as loud as a dog's bark.

TOKAY GECKO

Scientific name:	Gekko gecko
Size:	28 cm (11 in)
Range:	Asia, Indonesia
Habitat:	In or near houses

Chunky tail

Spotted body gives the lizard its name

Long legs hold body well off the ground when lizard runs

LEOPARD GECKO

Scientific name:	Eublepharius macularius
Size:	Up to 30 cm (12 in)
Range:	SW central Asia
Habitat:	Dry rocky regions

This night hunter preys on grasshoppers, scorpions, beetles and spiders. The leopard gecko is unusual because it has movable eyelids. Most geckos have fused, transparent eyelids and cannot blink.

KUHL'S GECKO

Scientific name:	*Ptychozoon kuhli*
Size:	15 cm (6 in)
Range:	SE Asia
Habitat:	Forest

Kuhl's gecko has webbed feet and flaps of skin along the sides of its body. It can glide from tree to tree, using the flaps and webbing like tiny parachutes.

There is little rain in the desert, so this lizard laps dew from rocks and even licks its own eyes to get vital moisture. Its body can also absorb water from mists and breezes that blow in from the sea.

WEB-FOOTED GECKO

Scientific name:	*Palmatogecko rangei*
Size:	12 cm (5 in)
Range:	Namib Desert, SW Africa
Habitat:	Sand dunes, rocks

Webbed feet spread the lizard's weight, enabling it to run quickly over the shifting desert sand

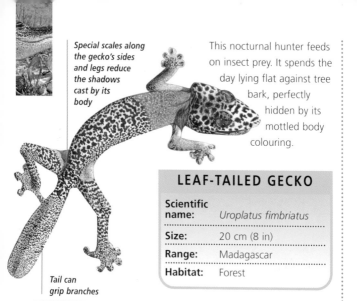

Special scales along the gecko's sides and legs reduce the shadows cast by its body

This nocturnal hunter feeds on insect prey. It spends the day lying flat against tree bark, perfectly hidden by its mottled body colouring.

Tail can grip branches

LEAF-TAILED GECKO

Scientific name:	*Uroplatus fimbriatus*
Size:	20 cm (8 in)
Range:	Madagascar
Habitat:	Forest

The eyes of this strange blind lizard are covered by scales. It spends its life burrowing in soil and rotting logs. It is limbless, but the male has tiny flipperlike stumps at the rear.

Wormlike body is ideal for burrowing

DIBAMUS NOVAEGUINEAE

Size:	30 cm (12 in)
Range:	New Guinea
Habitat:	Forest

When threatened, the scaly-foot mimics a poisonous snake, puffing out its throat, hissing and curling its neck into an S shape.

This limbless lizard hides in grass and plant litter, emerging to hunt insects and small lizards. It seizes prey with a snap of its jaws and swallows it whole.

BURTON'S SNAKE-LIZARD

Scientific name:	*Lialis burtonis*
Size:	Up to 61 cm (24 in)
Range:	Australia, New Guinea
Habitat:	Semi-desert, rainforest

Long wedge-shaped snout tapers to a point

PHELSUMA VINSONI

Size:	17 cm (7 in)
Range:	Mauritius
Habitat:	Forest

Males of the species are more brightly coloured than the females

This vividly patterned gecko is active during the day. It is an expert climber, scaling great heights in search of fruit and flower nectar.

The lizard gets its name because its hind legs consist of scaly flaps containing miniature leg and foot bones.

HOODED SCALY-FOOT

Scientific name:	*Pygopus nigriceps*
Size:	46 cm (18 in)
Range:	W Australia
Habitat:	Dry country, coastal forest

STRAND RACERUNNER

Scientific name:	*Cnemidophorus lemniscatus*
Size:	30 cm (12 in)
Range:	Central & South America
Habitat:	Forest, lowland plains

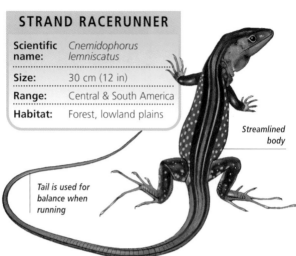

Streamlined body

Tail is used for balance when running

This agile lizard is constantly on the move, darting over the ground and reaching speeds of up to 28 km/h (17 mph) on its hind legs.

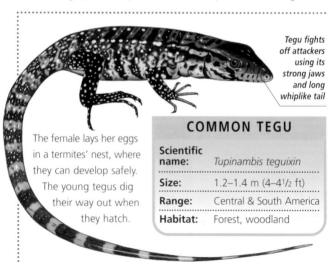

Tegu fights off attackers using its strong jaws and long whiplike tail

The female lays her eggs in a termites' nest, where they can develop safely. The young tegus dig their way out when they hatch.

COMMON TEGU

Scientific name:	*Tupinambis teguixin*
Size:	1.2–1.4 m (4–4½ ft)
Range:	Central & South America
Habitat:	Forest, woodland

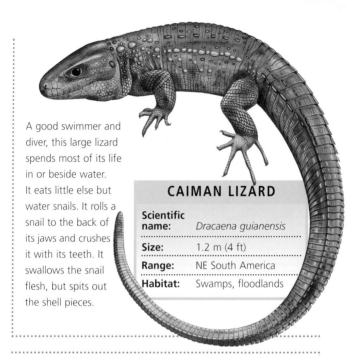

A good swimmer and diver, this large lizard spends most of its life in or beside water. It eats little else but water snails. It rolls a snail to the back of its jaws and crushes it with its teeth. It swallows the snail flesh, but spits out the shell pieces.

CAIMAN LIZARD

Scientific name:	*Dracaena guianensis*
Size:	1.2 m (4 ft)
Range:	NE South America
Habitat:	Swamps, floodlands

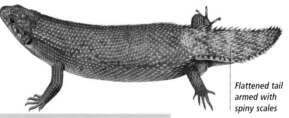

Flattened tail armed with spiny scales

SPINY-TAILED SKINK

Scientific name:	*Egernia stokesii*
Size:	Up to 27 cm (11 in)
Range:	Australia
Habitat:	Stony hills, mountains

This lizard curls its spine-clad tail round in front of its body to defend itself. It shelters in rock crevices, emerging to bask in the sun and forage for insects.

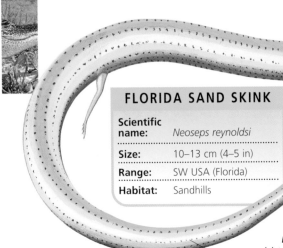

FLORIDA SAND SKINK

Scientific name:	Neoseps reynoldsi
Size:	10–13 cm (4–5 in)
Range:	SW USA (Florida)
Habitat:	Sandhills

Body and tail undulate as the skink "swims" through sand

GREAT PLAINS SKINK

Scientific name:	Eumeces obsoletus
Size:	16–35 cm (6–14 in)
Range:	C & SW USA, Mexico
Habitat:	Rocky grassland

The female Great Plains skink lays her eggs under a rock. She guards the eggs and helps the young babies hatch out. For 10 days after hatching, the mother looks after the young lizards, cleaning them regularly.

Sturdy legs

Rounded, tapering, smooth-scaled body, in common with most skinks

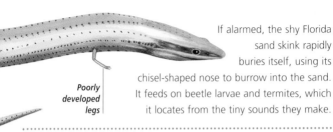

If alarmed, the shy Florida sand skink rapidly buries itself, using its chisel-shaped nose to burrow into the sand. It feeds on beetle larvae and termites, which it locates from the tiny sounds they make.

Poorly developed legs

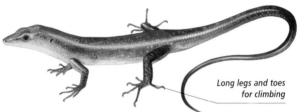

Long legs and toes for climbing

This tree lizard often forages for food on the ground, but spends most of the day basking on branches or sheltering under banana leaves.

EMOIA CYANOGASTER

Size:	Up to 27 cm (11 in)
Range:	NW Australia, Indonesia
Habitat:	Forest, banana groves

Limbless cylindrical body

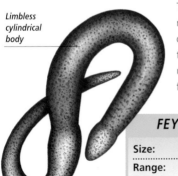

This burrowing skink has no external eardrums and only tiny eyes protected by transparent scales. It lurks under rotting wood and feeds mainly on termites.

FEYLINIA CUSSORI

Size:	35 cm (14 in)
Range:	Tropical Africa
Habitat:	Forest

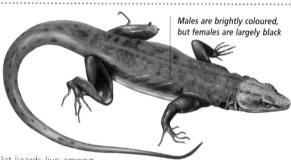

Skin colour varies in different parts of Europe

Long tapering tail may be up to twice as long as the body

WALL LIZARD

Scientific name:	*Podarcis muralis*
Size:	Up to 23 cm (9 in)
Range:	C & S Europe
Habitat:	Dry sunny areas

An expert climber, this sun-loving lizard is often seen basking in large numbers on walls and buildings or beside the road. It eats insects, slugs, snails, worms and spiders.

Males are brightly coloured, but females are largely black

Flat lizards live among rocks. Their bodies are only about 1 cm ($^3/_8$ in) thick, allowing them to squeeze into narrow rock crevices. Females lay their eggs in a communal nest, usually a crevice filled with damp plant litter.

IMPERIAL FLAT LIZARD

Scientific name:	*Platysaurus imperator*
Size:	39 cm (15 in)
Range:	SE Africa
Habitat:	Rocky grassland

This lizard spends the day sheltering under the dead leaves of plants such as yucca and agave, emerging at night to hunt beetles, ants, termites and flies.

The female desert night lizard does not lay eggs, but gives birth to live young, which develop inside her body.

Tail can easily be discarded to escape danger

DESERT NIGHT LIZARD

Scientific name:	*Xantusia vigilis*
Size:	9–12 cm (3½–5 in)
Range:	SW USA
Habitat:	Rocky dry country

ARMADILLO LIZARD

Scientific name:	*Cordylus cataphractus*
Size:	21 cm (8 in)
Range:	South Africa
Habitat:	Dry rocky areas

This armour-plated lizard curls up into a ball when threatened to protect its soft belly – its only weak spot. Would-be predators are left facing a formidable ring of sharp spiny scales.

Belly area is soft

Spiny scales cover upper body

Tail wraps around branches

Lizard readily bites attackers

SOUTHERN ALLIGATOR LIZARD

Scientific name:	*Gerrhonotus multicarinatus*
Size:	25–43 cm (10–17 in)
Range:	W USA, Mexico
Habitat:	Grassland, woodland

The alligator lizard uses its grasping tail to help it climb shrubs and trees in search of insects and newly hatched birds. It also forages on the ground in plant litter for scorpions, slugs and spiders – even venomous black widows.

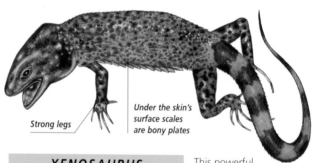

Strong legs

Under the skin's surface scales are bony plates

XENOSAURUS

Size:	About 20 cm (8 in)
Range:	Mexico, Guatemala
Habitat:	Rainforest

This powerful lizard is rarely seen, as it spends most of its time sheltering under tree roots or in rock crevices. It eats termites and ants.

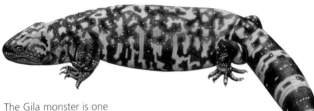

The Gila monster is one of only two venomous lizards, but its bite is rarely fatal to humans. It preys on birds, mice and other lizards. If food is scarce, it can survive for several months on the fat stored in its thick tail.

GILA MONSTER

Scientific name:	*Heloderma suspectum*
Size:	45–61cm (18–24 in)
Range:	SW USA
Habitat:	Desert, semi-desert

SLOW WORM

Scientific name:	*Anguis fragilis*
Size:	35–54 cm (14–21 in)
Range:	Europe, W Asia, N Africa
Habitat:	Fields, meadows, scrub

Slow worms live longer than many other lizards. One captive slow worm reached the age of 54.

Slow worm moves its long smooth body like a snake

Slow worms spend the night and the heat of the day under logs or rocks. They are voracious feeders on slugs, snails, worms and insects.

Huge claws for excavating burrows and climbing trees

NILE MONITOR

Scientific name:	*Varanus niloticus*
Size:	Over 2 m (6½ ft)
Range:	SE Africa
Habitat:	Forest, open country

Nile monitors live near water, feeding on frogs, fish and snails. They also raid crocodile nests, digging out the eggs and eating them.

Tongue tastes the air

Lizard rears up tall to survey the land, using its tail as a "third leg"

Strong legs

GOULD'S MONITOR

Scientific name:	*Varanus gouldi*
Size:	About 1.5 m (5 ft)
Range:	Australia
Habitat:	Coastal forest, desert

Gould's monitor wanders over huge areas as it searches for mammals, reptiles, birds and insects to eat. It often shelters in a burrow, which it either digs itself or takes over from another animal.

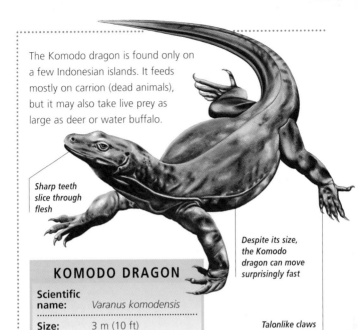

The Komodo dragon is found only on a few Indonesian islands. It feeds mostly on carrion (dead animals), but it may also take live prey as large as deer or water buffalo.

Sharp teeth slice through flesh

Despite its size, the Komodo dragon can move surprisingly fast

Talonlike claws are used for digging and for disembowelling prey

KOMODO DRAGON

Scientific name:	*Varanus komodensis*
Size:	3 m (10 ft)
Range:	Indonesia
Habitat:	Grassland

On land and in water, the lizard moves by wriggling its body from side to side

Tiny eyes

This lizard uses its head to burrow through soil. When not underground, it is usually swimming in swamps or murky ditches. It rarely moves on land.

EARLESS MONITOR

Scientific name:	*Lanthanotus borneensis*
Size:	Up to 43 cm (17 in)
Range:	Borneo
Habitat:	Forest, swamp

Worm lizards

Despite their name, these strange burrowing reptiles are not true lizards. They spend most of their lives underground, building tunnels by battering through soil with their hard heads.

Worm lizard moves through tunnels by contracting and relaxing the muscles along the length of its body

Tail is the same shape as the head

Tail is waved about to distract predators, allowing worm lizard to counterattack

This worm lizard is often found inside the huge nests of leaf-cutter ants, where it is thought to lay its eggs. It eats just about any animal it can overpower.

Interlocking teeth set in powerful jaws tear apart prey such as earthworms and ants

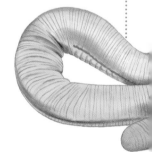

WHITE-BELLIED WORM LIZARD

Scientific name:	*Amphisbaena alba*
Size:	61 cm (24 in)
Range:	Tropical South America
Habitat:	Rainforest

SOMALI EDGE SNOUT

Scientific name:	*Agamodon anguliceps*
Size:	11 cm (4 in)
Range:	E Africa
Habitat:	Sandy soil

Like all worm lizards, the edge snout detects insect prey from the vibrations they make as they move through the soil. It moves close to the surface at night, but digs deeper in the heat of the day.

Special wedge-shaped snout has sharp vertical ridges to tackle hard soil

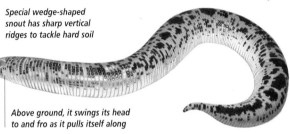

Above ground, it swings its head to and fro as it pulls itself along

Skin hangs loosely around the body, which is ringed with small scales

TWO-LEGGED WORM LIZARD

Scientific name:	*Bipes biporus*
Size:	20 cm (8 in)
Range:	NW Mexico
Habitat:	Semi-desert

This unusual worm lizard has two tiny but powerful front legs, with five clawed toes on each. The worm lizard uses the legs to start digging its tunnels and push soil behind it as it burrows.

Snakes

Snakes are legless reptiles with long thin bodies. They eat meat and swallow their prey whole. They have forked tongues, but they do not have ear openings or movable eyelids.

RED-BLOTCHED SHIELDTAIL

Scientific name:	*Uropeltis biomaculatus*
Size:	Up to 30 cm (12 in)
Range:	India, Sri Lanka
Habitat:	Mountain forest

Microscopic ridges on the scales scatter light in all directions, giving the skin a shimmering appearance

The red-blotched shieldtail sometimes climbs trees

This secretive burrowing snake feeds mostly on earthworms. It has a single large spiked scale at the end of its tail, which gives the snake its name. The scale wards off pursuing predators as the shieldtail burrows forwards.

Tail spike is pushed into the soil to steady the snake as it burrows

Smooth, thin, cylindrical body is ideal for tunnelling

Blind snakes are burrowers. Their tiny eyes are almost useless underground, so they locate ants, termites and other insect prey by scent. A blind snake digs with its head, which is protected by large tough scales.

SCHLEGEL'S BLIND SNAKE

Scientific name:	*Typhlops schlegelii*
Size:	60 cm (24 in)
Range:	Kenya to South Africa
Habitat:	Sandy or loamy soil

This beautiful shiny snake lives both above and below ground. It burrows rapidly in soft soil using its wedge-shaped head. It eats frogs, lizards, small rodents and other snakes.

SUNBEAM SNAKE

Scientific name:	*Xenopeltis unicolor*
Size:	Up to 1 m (3¼ ft)
Range:	SE Asia
Habitat:	Farmland

Muscular body encircles prey

Skin is covered by smooth shiny scales

Like all constricting snakes, boas kill their prey, such as birds and mammals, by wrapping their strong bodies around victims and squeezing hard until they suffocate.

BOA CONSTRICTOR

Scientific name:	*Boa constrictor*
Size:	Up to 5.6 m (18½ ft)
Range:	Central & South America
Habitat:	Desert to rainforest

RUBBER BOA

Scientific name:	*Charina bottae*
Size:	35–84 cm (14–33 in)
Range:	W USA
Habitat:	Forest, grassland

At night, this constrictor emerges from its burrow or from under rocks or logs to hunt salamanders, shrews, mice and snakes. If disturbed, it rolls itself up into a very tight ball.

Skin feels rubbery, which gives the snake its name

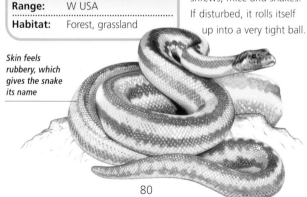

EMERALD TREE BOA

Scientific name:	*Boa caninus*
Size:	1.2 m (4 ft)
Range:	C South America
Habitat:	Rainforest

Body loops around branches when snake is resting

When resting or lying in wait for prey, the body of this tree-dwelling constrictor is anchored firmly to a branch by its gripping tail. The snake preys on lizards, birds and small mammals, which it ambushes in the treetops.

The mouth of this burrowing snake does not open wide, so it can only eat slender prey, such as other snakes, worm lizards and legless amphibians known as caecilians.

FALSE CORAL SNAKE

Scientific name:	*Anilius scytale*
Size:	75–85 cm (30–33 in)
Range:	N South America
Habitat:	Forest

Colouring is thought to mimic that of the venomous coral snakes

ELEPHANT-TRUNK SNAKE

Tiny touch-sensitive hairs on the surface of each lumpy scale detect prey in murky water

Scientific name:	*Acrochordus javanicus*
Size:	1.5 m (5 ft)
Range:	S Asia, New Guinea
Habitat:	Rivers, canals, estuaries

This snake coils up its body in the water to make itself resemble a rock or tree stump. Fish coming to shelter or look for food in its inviting nooks and crannies are seized and swallowed.

The anaconda often lurks in muddy water. It seizes animals that come to the water's edge to drink, and kills them by constriction.

ANACONDA

Scientific name:	*Eunectes murinus*
Size:	9 m (29½ ft)
Range:	South America
Habitat:	Swamps, riverbanks

Only the head breaks the surface when the anaconda is in water

The anaconda is one of the world's longest snakes.

This large constrictor prowls at night for mice, wild boar, deer and other prey. The female curls around her clutch of up to 100 eggs until they hatch.

INDIAN PYTHON

Scientific name:	*Python molurus*
Size:	5–6.1 m (16½–20 ft)
Range:	India, SE Asia
Habitat:	Swamp, scrub, rainforest

In some places, Indian pythons are under threat because people hunt them for their skins.

This venomous snake uses the huge fangs in its shovel-shaped head to kill prey such as burrowing lizards and blind snakes. It spends most of its time below ground, digging through soil with its strong pointed snout.

BIBRON'S BURROWING ASP

Scientific name:	*Atractaspis bibroni*
Size:	Up to 80 cm (32 in)
Range:	South Africa
Habitat:	Dry sandy regions

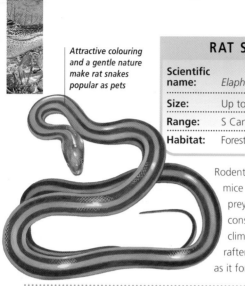

Attractive colouring and a gentle nature make rat snakes popular as pets

RAT SNAKE

Scientific name:	*Elaphe obsoleta*
Size:	Up to 2.5 m (8¼ ft)
Range:	S Canada to N Mexico
Habitat:	Forests, swamp, farmland

Rodents such as rats and mice are the favourite prey of this powerful constrictor. It often climbs up on to the rafters of farm buildings as it forages for food.

This water snake forages for small crabs among the roots of mangrove trees on coastal mud flats. It also eats some fish. When alarmed, it hides in a crab burrow.

WHITE-BELLIED MANGROVE SNAKE

Scientific name:	*Fordonia leucobalia*
Size:	Up to 1 m (3¼ ft)
Range:	N Australia, SE Asia
Habitat:	Mangrove swamps

Nostrils high up on the skull allow the snake to breathe with its body under water and just the top of its head showing

PARADISE TREE SNAKE

Scientific name:	*Chrysopelea paradisi*
Size:	Up to 1.2 m (4 ft)
Range:	Philippines to Indonesia
Habitat:	Forest

This snake is a superb climber and spends most of its time in the trees. It can launch itself into the air from a branch and glide 20 m (65 ft) or more to a safe landing on another tree. However, it cannot steer itself as it glides.

The snake spreads out its ribs when it glides, curving its body so that it acts like a parachute

COMMON KINGSNAKE

Scientific name:	*Lampropeltis geltulus*
Size:	90 cm–2 m (35 in–6½ ft)
Range:	USA, Mexico
Habitat:	Most types

Kingsnakes are famous for eating other snakes, including coral snakes and rattlesnakes. They also eat birds, mice and lizards, killing them by constriction.

The spotted water snake kills its prey with a bite from venomous fangs at the back of its upper jaw.

SPOTTED WATER SNAKE

Scientific name:	*Enhydris punctata*
Size:	30–50 cm (12–20 in)
Range:	N Australia
Habitat:	Creeks, swamps, rivers

Upward-pointing eyes

Nostrils close under water

The spotted water snake hunts fish, frogs and other aquatic animals. It leaves the water to bask on riverbanks and shores.

EGG-EATING SNAKE

Scientific name:	*Dasypeltis scabra*
Size:	75 cm (30 in)
Range:	S & E Africa
Habitat:	Woodland, scrub

This slender snake eats only birds' eggs. An egg is swallowed whole. The shell is pierced by spikes in the snake's neck and strong muscles squeeze out the contents of the egg. The snake coughs up the pieces of shell.

This snake's long thin greeny-brown body hides it well among vines and creepers as it rests on the branches of rainforest trees. It feeds on young birds, which it snatches from nests, and lizards.

VINE SNAKE

Scientific name:	*Oxybelis fulgidus*
Size:	1.5–2 m (5–6½ ft)
Range:	Central & South America
Habitat:	Rainforest, farmland

Body is just 1.25 cm (½ in) in diameter

In the breeding season, the male grass snake courts the female by rubbing his chin over her body before mating. The female lays 30 to 40 eggs in a warm place, often among rotting vegetation.

GRASS SNAKE

Scientific name:	*Natrix natrix*
Size:	1.2–2 m (4–6½ ft)
Range:	Europe, N Africa, W Asia
Habitat:	Pond edges, riverbanks

The grass snake swims well. It hunts fish and frogs in rivers, as well as small mammals on land. Most of its prey is swallowed alive.

Flattened body helps snake move more easily through the water

Paddle-shaped tail

BANDED SEA SNAKE

Scientific name:	*Hydrophis cyanocinctus*
Size:	2 m (6½ ft)
Range:	Indian & Pacific oceans
Habitat:	Coastal waters

This snake never leaves the water and even gives birth at sea. It can stay under water for up to two hours without coming up for air.

Red-bellies are popular with blueberry farmers because they prey on slugs that damage fruit crops. They also eat snails, earthworms and insects.

RED-BELLIED SNAKE

Scientific name:	*Storeria occipitomaculata*
Size:	20–40 cm (8–16 in)
Range:	S Canada, E USA
Habitat:	Hilly woodland, bogs

When alarmed, the snake curls its upper lip, exposing the black lining of its mouth and the teeth on its upper jaw.

COMMON GARTER SNAKE

Scientific name:	*Thamnophis sirtalis*
Size:	Up to 91 cm (36 in)
Range:	S Canada, USA
Habitat:	Fields, woodland

The common garter snake likes moist places and is often found in wet meadows, beside streams and even in drainage ditches. It slithers through damp vegetation searching for prey such as salamanders, frogs, toads and earthworms. The female gives birth to as many as 50 live young.

Stripes resemble the pattern on old-fashioned garters, which were used to hold up stockings

Long slender body

MANGROVE SNAKE

Scientific name:	*Boiga dendrophila*
Size:	2.5 m (8 1/4 ft)
Range:	Philippines to Indonesia
Habitat:	Rainforest, mangroves

The mangrove snake spends most of its life in trees overhanging rivers, streams and swamps. At dusk, it sets off to hunt frogs and other animals.

Pattern hides snake amid light and shade of forest trees

"Eye" marks confuse enemies

EGYPTIAN COBRA

Scientific name:	*Naja haje*
Size:	Up to 2.6 m (8½ ft)
Range:	Africa
Habitat:	Savanna

Ribs of the neck spread out to pull the loose skin into a hood shape

When threatened, this nocturnal snake makes itself look more fearsome by raising the front of its body and spreading the loose skin around its neck to form a hood shape. Some cobra species can spray a jet of venom up to 2 m (6½ ft) into the eyes of an attacker, causing great pain.

KING COBRA

Cobra's head may be as big as a man's hand

Scientific name:	*Ophiophagus hannah*
Size:	4–5.5 m (13–18 ft)
Range:	S Asia to Philippines
Habitat:	Forest

The king cobra, the world's largest venomous snake, feeds mostly on lizards and other snakes. The female builds a nest out of leaves and twigs in which to lay her eggs.

90

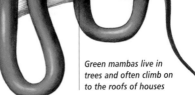

Mambas are among the fastest moving of all snakes

Green mambas live in trees and often climb on to the roofs of houses

This snake has highly toxic venom, but it rarely bites humans and prefers to flee from danger or threats. In the breeding season, the males fight over females. They entwine their bodies and threaten each other with raised heads.

EASTERN GREEN MAMBA

Scientific name:	*Dendroaspis angusticeps*
Size:	2 m (6½ ft)
Range:	E & S Africa
Habitat:	Savanna

After sheltering from the heat of the day, this snake emerges at night to stalk lizards and frogs. It is very aggressive and bites readily.

DE VIS'S BANDED SNAKE

Scientific name:	*Denisonia devisii*
Size:	50 cm (20 in)
Range:	W Australia
Habitat:	Dry wooded areas

SAW-SCALED ADDER

Scientific name:	Echis carinatus
Size:	53–72 cm (21–28 in)
Range:	N Africa, SW Asia
Habitat:	Dry sandy regions

To threaten enemies, this highly venomous snake coils up its body and rubs its sawlike scales over each other to make a loud rasping noise.

Heat-sensitive pits on snout detect body heat of prey

The bite of this pit viper causes more human deaths than any other snake in South America. The fangs are housed in a fleshy sheath that pulls back as the snake bites.

FER-DE-LANCE

Scientific name:	Bothrops atrox
Size:	2.45 m (8 ft)
Range:	Mexico to South America
Habitat:	Low coastal areas

The puff adder is one of the biggest vipers, with a body up to 23 cm (9 in) across. Before it strikes with its fangs, it puffs itself with air so it looks even larger.

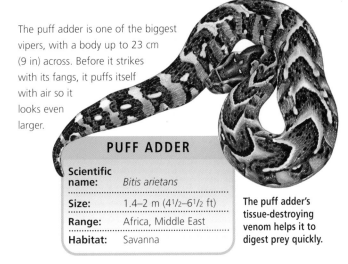

PUFF ADDER

Scientific name:	*Bitis arietans*
Size:	1.4–2 m (4½–6½ ft)
Range:	Africa, Middle East
Habitat:	Savanna

The puff adder's tissue-destroying venom helps it to digest prey quickly.

GABOON VIPER

Scientific name:	*Bitis gabonica*
Size:	1.2–2 m (4–6½ ft)
Range:	W & SW Africa
Habitat:	Rainforest

The Gaboon viper's fangs measure up to 5 cm (2 in) long – the longest of any viper. The strong venom they inject into prey causes severe bleeding. It also affects the victim's breathing and heartbeat.

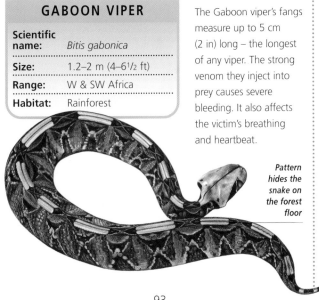

Pattern hides the snake on the forest floor

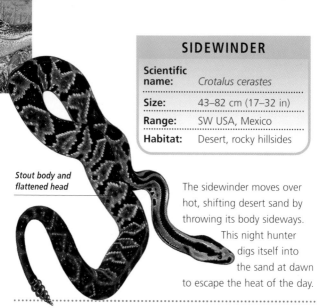

SIDEWINDER

Scientific name:	*Crotalus cerastes*
Size:	43–82 cm (17–32 in)
Range:	SW USA, Mexico
Habitat:	Desert, rocky hillsides

Stout body and flattened head

The sidewinder moves over hot, shifting desert sand by throwing its body sideways. This night hunter digs itself into the sand at dawn to escape the heat of the day.

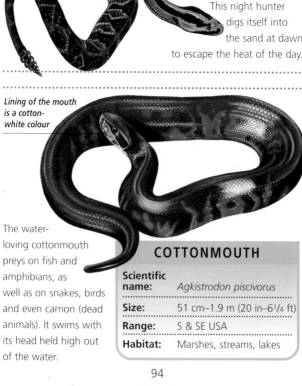

Lining of the mouth is a cotton-white colour

The water-loving cottonmouth preys on fish and amphibians, as well as on snakes, birds and even carrion (dead animals). It swims with its head held high out of the water.

COTTONMOUTH

Scientific name:	*Agkistrodon piscivorus*
Size:	51 cm–1.9 m (20 in–6¼ ft)
Range:	S & SE USA
Habitat:	Marshes, streams, lakes

The venom of the diamondback attacks the blood cells of its victim.

Tail rattle

EASTERN DIAMONDBACK

Scientific name:	*Crotalus adamanteus*
Size:	1–2.4 m (3¼–7¾ ft)
Range:	E USA
Habitat:	Woodland, farmland

Like all rattlesnakes, the eastern diamondback, when threatened, can make a rattling sound by shaking the hollow rings at the tip of its tail. The sound may also lure prey.

Bushmasters ambush passing prey. This sit-and-wait hunting method uses little energy, so the snake does not need to feed very often – perhaps only every two to three weeks.

BUSHMASTER

Scientific name:	*Lachesis muta*
Size:	2.45–3.5 m (8–11½ ft)
Range:	Central & South America
Habitat:	Rainforest

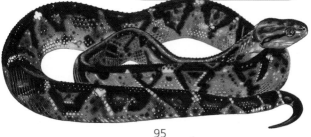

Chelonians

The bodies of these reptiles are protected by bony shells. Chelonians that spend most or all of their time in water are known as turtles or terrapins. Land-dwellers are called tortoises.

Shell pattern hides tortoise among plant litter

Chelonians have good eyesight

This tortoise has a unique shell, with a special hinge that allows the rear part to be lowered if the tortoise is attacked from behind. The hingeback eats plants and occasionally catches small animals.

SERRATED HINGEBACK TORTOISE

Scientific name:	*Kinixys erosa*
Size:	33 cm (13 in)
Range:	W & C Africa
Habitat:	Rainforest, marshes

BOWSPRIT TORTOISE

Scientific name:	*Chersine angulata*
Size:	15–18 cm (6–7 in)
Range:	South Africa
Habitat:	Coastal areas

In August, the female bowsprit digs a hole 10 cm (4 in) deep and lays 1 or 2 eggs in it. The eggs hatch about a year later.

The front opening of the bowsprit's shell extends over the tortoise's neck, providing good protection against attacks from predators.

Distinctive triangular pattern

Some Galápagos tortoises can live for up to 150 years.

GALÁPAGOS GIANT TORTOISE

Scientific name:	*Geochelone nigra*
Size:	Up to 1.2 m (4 ft)
Range:	Galápagos Islands
Habitat:	Varied

These lumbering giants can weigh up to 385 kg (850 lb). They eat whatever plants they can find. In dry periods, they get the water they need by eating cactuses – including the spikes! Some have a shell that curves up at the front, so that the tortoise can stretch its neck up to reach high leaves.

97

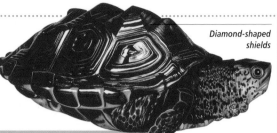

Diamond-shaped shields

DIAMONDBACK TERRAPIN

Scientific name:	*Malaclemys terrapin*
Size:	10–23 cm (4–9 in)
Range:	W coast of USA
Habitat:	Salt marshes, estuaries

The diamondback feeds on snails, clams, worms and plant shoots by day, and buries itself in mud at night. It lives in salty water, but it still needs to be near a source of fresh water for drinking.

A box turtle may eat mushrooms that are toxic to humans. Anyone who then eats the turtle will be poisoned.

Turtle can withdraw its whole body into its shell

EASTERN BOX TURTLE

Scientific name:	*Terrapene carolina*
Size:	10–20 cm (4–8 in)
Range:	E & SE USA
Habitat:	Moist forested regions

The box turtle spends most of its time on land. It is a poor swimmer, so when it enters water it keeps to the shallows. It may take refuge from the summer heat in swampy areas.

The pancake tortoise has a flat, flexible shell that allows it to hide from danger by squeezing into gaps between rocks. By slightly puffing up its body, it can resist being dragged out again by a predator. Pancake tortoises eat dry grass.

AFRICAN PANCAKE TORTOISE

Scientific name:	*Malocochersus tornieri*
Size:	15 cm (6 in)
Range:	Kenya, Tanzania
Habitat:	Dry rocky outcrops

Especially light shell enables the tortoise to move quickly

SPUR-THIGHED TORTOISE

Scientific name:	*Testudo gracea*
Size:	15 cm (6 in)
Range:	Mediterranean region
Habitat:	Dry scrubland

Spur-thighed tortoises are rare because millions were captured and sold as pets. Some trade still goes on, but it is now banned in most countries.

This tortoise gets its name from the small spur on the thigh of each front leg. During courtship, the male butts and bites the female before the pair mates.

Domed shell

River terrapins may migrate over 100 km (60 miles) to find a nesting site. Their numbers are falling because people often kill them for food.

RIVER TERRAPIN

Scientific name:	*Batagur baska*
Size:	58 cm (23 in)
Range:	SE Asia
Habitat:	Tidal areas, estuaries

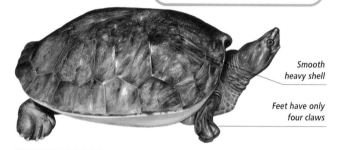

Smooth heavy shell

Feet have only four claws

After mating, the female false map turtle finds a sunny spot beside water and digs a pit in the soil with her rear feet. She lays her clutch of 6 to 15 eggs and then covers them with soil to bury them.

FALSE MAP TURTLE

Scientific name:	*Graptemys pseudogeographica*
Size:	8–25 cm (3–10 in)
Range:	NC to SC USA
Habitat:	Rivers, lakes, ponds

Intricately patterned shell

The male drums on the female's snout with his claws during courtship.

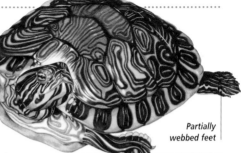

These turtles slide rapidly into the water when disturbed.

Partially webbed feet

Pond sliders stay close to water and often bask on floating logs. Young pond sliders catch prey such as insects, tadpoles and snails, but adults eat mainly plants. Females lay up to 70 eggs a year.

POND SLIDER

Scientific name:	*Trachemys scripta*
Size:	13–30 cm (5–12 in)
Range:	SE USA to Brazil
Habitat:	Rivers, ponds, swamps

To avoid the cold winter weather, this turtle hibernates under mud or in a chamber that it digs in the riverbank.

EUROPEAN POND TURTLE

Scientific name:	*Emys orbicularis*
Size:	13–15 cm (5–6 in)
Range:	S Europe, N Africa to Iran
Habitat:	Ponds, marshes, rivers

The European pond turtle eats fish, frogs, snails and worms.

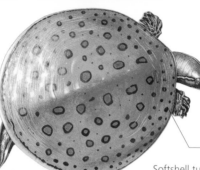

Snorkel-like nose for breathing under water

Small spines round the front edge of the shell

SPINY SOFTSHELL

Scientific name:	*Trionyx spiniferus*
Size:	15–46 cm (6–18 in)
Range:	E North America
Habitat:	Rivers, creeks, ponds

Softshell turtles have bendy, rounded shells with no hard plates in them. The spiny softshell can move fast on land and in water. It eats insects, crayfish, fish and plants. In summer, the female lays about 20 eggs.

INDIAN SOFTSHELL

Scientific name:	*Chitra indica*
Size:	91 cm (36 in)
Range:	India, Pakistan, Thailand
Habitat:	Rivers

A lover of sandy river bottoms, this turtle has an unusually long neck and eyes placed far forwards near its snout. Its flipperlike limbs make it a fast swimmer. Molluscs and fish are its favourite prey.

YELLOW MUD TURTLE

Scientific name:	*Kinosternon flavescens*
Size:	9–16 cm (3½–6 in)
Range:	C & SC USA
Habitat:	Slow streams

This turtle prefers muddy streams, but it may also be found in ditches and cattle troughs. It pulls its head back into its shell when danger threatens.

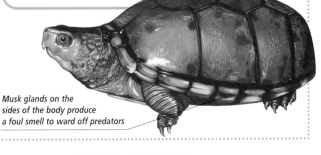

Musk glands on the sides of the body produce a foul smell to ward off predators

NEW GUINEA PLATELESS TURTLE

Scientific name:	*Carettochelys insculpta*
Size:	46 cm (18 in)
Range:	New Guinea
Habitat:	Rivers

With its flattened shell and paddle-shaped limbs, this turtle is well suited to life in water. The female lays 17 to 27 eggs. The hatchlings are 6 cm (2½ in) long.

Limbs are like those of a sea turtle

Flattened shell cuts easily through water

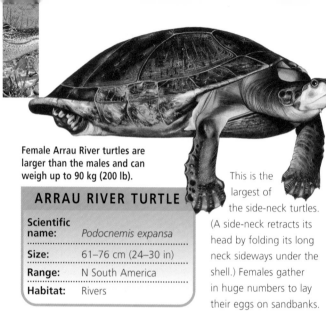

Female Arrau River turtles are larger than the males and can weigh up to 90 kg (200 lb).

ARRAU RIVER TURTLE

Scientific name:	*Podocnemis expansa*
Size:	61–76 cm (24–30 in)
Range:	N South America
Habitat:	Rivers

This is the largest of the side-neck turtles. (A side-neck retracts its head by folding its long neck sideways under the shell.) Females gather in huge numbers to lay their eggs on sandbanks.

The Murray River turtle is a side-neck

A newly hatched Murray River turtle has a circular shell. The shell gets wider at the back as the turtle grows. By the time it is an adult, the shell is oval shaped. It feeds on frogs, tadpoles and plants.

MURRAY RIVER TURTLE

Scientific name:	*Emydura macquarri*
Size:	30 cm (12 in)
Range:	SE Australia
Habitat:	Rivers

Notch in shell allows thick neck to be raised

Head is half the width of the shell

This turtle's head is too large to be retracted under its shell, so it has a bony roof to protect the brain. It uses long claws to climb over branches and rocks in search of food and good basking spots.

BIG-HEADED TURTLE

Scientific name:	*Platysternon megacephalum*
Size:	15–18 cm (6–7 in)
Range:	Burma, Thailand, S China
Habitat:	Mountain streams, rivers

SNAPPING TURTLE

Scientific name:	*Chelydra serpentina*
Size:	20–47 cm (8–19 in)
Range:	S Canada to Ecuador
Habitat:	Marshes, lakes, rivers

Hidden among water plants on the bottom, this turtle lies in wait for fish and frogs, then shoots its head forwards and snatches them in its strong jaws. It also preys on mammals and birds at the waterside.

Shell has a serrated edge and extremely thick horny plates

HAWKSBILL

Scientific name:	*Eretmochelys imbricata*
Size:	76–91 cm (30–36 in)
Range:	Tropical areas of Atlantic, Pacific & Indian oceans; Caribbean

The hawksbill has long been hunted for its striking shell, as well as for its eggs. It probes with its tapering snout among rocky crevices and coral reefs, looking for crustaceans, molluscs and sponges to eat.

Jaws crush prey such as shrimps, crabs and fish

Small lightly built body

Every year, female ridleys return to the same nesting beaches, often coming ashore by the thousand. Each lays up to 100 eggs in the sand, covers them, and then goes back to sea for another year.

PACIFIC RIDLEY

Scientific name:	*Lepidochelys olivacea*
Size:	66 cm (26 in)
Range:	Tropical areas of Indian, Pacific & S Atlantic oceans

Scientific name:	*Dermochelys coriacea*
Size:	1.5 m (5 ft)
Range:	Seas and oceans throughout the world

Weighing a hefty 360 kg (800 lb), the leatherback is the world's largest turtle. It is usually found in warm seas and feeds mainly on jellyfish. Each year, it travels vast distances at sea as it moves between its feeding and nesting sites.

Thick, leathery shell lacks horny shields, and the skin has no scales

Scissorlike jaws are very weak

Heavy clawless flippers

The wide chunky head of this marine turtle may be up to 25 cm (10 in) across. Its shell tapers towards the back, perhaps to protect it from attacks by sharks. Many are accidentally caught in fishing nets in coastal areas.

LOGGERHEAD TURTLE

Scientific name:	*Caretta caretta*
Size:	76 cm–1 m (30 in–3/4 ft)
Range:	Temperate and tropical areas of Indian, Pacific & Atlantic oceans

Strong jaws can crunch even hard-shelled clams

Crocodilians

These armoured reptiles are covered in horny scales called scutes and have bony plates in their backs for extra protection. Crocodilians have short legs and long powerful tails.

AMERICAN ALLIGATOR	
Scientific name:	*Aligator mississipiensis*
Size:	Up to 5.5 m (18 ft)
Range:	SE USA
Habitat:	Marshes, rivers, swamps

During courtship, the male strokes the female's body with his front legs, rubs her throat with his head and even blows bubbles past her cheeks.

Scutes in back contain small bones

The American alligator usually hunts in the cool of early evening. Its prey includes fish, turtles, snakes and mammals. It will sometimes rear up suddenly on its powerful tail to snatch birds perching on branches overhanging the water.

The gavial's long narrow snout is studded with about 100 small pointed teeth – ideal for seizing slippery fish and frogs. It catches prey by sweeping its snout sideways through the water.

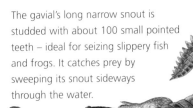

Legs are weak, so gavial moves poorly on land

GAVIAL

Scientific name:	*Gavialis gangeticus*
Size:	7 m (23 ft)
Range:	Pakistan to Bangladesh
Habitat:	Deep pools in large rivers

SPECTACLED CAIMAN

Scientific name:	*Caiman crocodilus*
Size:	1.5–2 m (5–6½ ft)
Range:	S Mexico to N Argentina
Habitat:	Swamps, rivers, lakes

The ridge between this crocodilian's eyes makes it look as if it is wearing glasses. The female guards her nest of up to 40 eggs against egg-stealing tegu lizards.

Nile crocodiles spend the night in water and come out on to the riverbank just before dawn to bask in the sun during the day. Adults swallow stones that act as ballast and help to keep their bodies balanced in the water.

Muscular tail propels crocodile through the water

NILE CROCODILE

Scientific name:	*Crocodylus niloticus*
Size:	4.5–5 m (14³/₄–16¹/₂ ft)
Range:	Africa
Habitat:	Rivers, lakes, marshes

MUGGER

Scientific name:	*Crocodylus palustris*
Size:	Up to 4 m (13 ft)
Range:	Indian subcontinent
Habitat:	Marshes, lakes, rivers

To attract females, male muggers make a loud echoing noise by smacking their jaws on the water's surface.

Broad snout

Muggers prefer shallow water less than 5 m (16¹/₂ ft) deep. They eat a wide range of prey, including deer, frogs, snakes, turtles and insects. Some have learned to steal fish from nets.

Little is known about this shy, slow-moving animal. It hunts crabs, frogs and fish at night. It spends most of its time alone, except when pairs come together to mate.

WEST AFRICAN DWARF CROCODILE

Scientific name:	*Osteolaemus tetraspis*
Size:	1.5 m (5 ft)
Range:	W & SW Africa
Habitat:	Streams, lakes, swamps

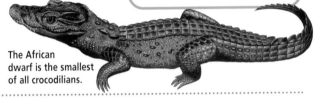

The African dwarf is the smallest of all crocodilians.

ESTUARINE CROCODILE

Scientific name:	*Crocodylus porosus*
Size:	Up to 6 m (20 ft)
Range:	S Asia to N Australia
Habitat:	Estuaries, coasts

This crocodile is known to attack people who enter its territory, especially in the mating and nesting seasons. It catches fish at sea, but it will also eat birds and land animals such as buffalo.

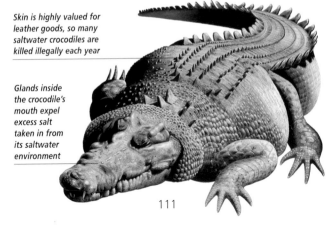

Skin is highly valued for leather goods, so many saltwater crocodiles are killed illegally each year

Glands inside the crocodile's mouth expel excess salt taken in from its saltwater environment

Glossary

adapted The way an animal has developed special features to enable it to survive in a particular habitat.

amnion A bag of fluid that cushions a reptile embryo inside an egg.

amphibian An animal such as a frog, toad, salamander or newt. Amphibians are cold-blooded, have moist skin and usually live in damp habitats. Most young amphibians are aquatic and have gills, but later change into air-breathing adults.

ancestor A plant or animal from which a later form of plant or animal evolved.

aquatic Living most or all of the time in water.

ballast Something used to weigh down a floating object and keep it steady in the water.

bask To lie in the sunshine for warmth.

camouflage The way that an animal's colour, patterning or shape helps it to blend in with its surroundings, so that it is hidden from view.

carnivores Animals that eat meat.

carrion Dead animal flesh.

cells The microscopic building blocks from which all living things are made. A plant or animal contains many different types of cells, which carry out a wide variety of tasks.

chelonian A shelled reptile such as a turtle or tortoise.

cloaca The chamber inside the bodies of reptiles, fish and amphibians into which the sexual organs, digestive system and bladder empty.

cold-blooded An animal that is not able to keep a constant body temperature. Its body temperature depends on the temperature of its surroundings. Cold-blooded reptiles bask in the sun to warm up, and shelter from the sun to cool down.

communal Used by many animals.

constrictor A snake that kills prey by coiling round it and squeezing it until it suffocates.

courtship Animal behaviour that leads to the selection of a mate and to mating.

crocodilian A crocodile, alligator, caiman or gavial.

den An animal's home. Some snakes gather in large numbers to hibernate in dens.

desert A region with extremely low rainfall. Deserts can be very hot or very cold.

dinosaurs A group of reptiles that dominated the Earth 230 to 65 million years ago before dying out suddenly. The name dinosaur means "terrible lizard".

dominant A dominant animal is the one that rules in a group or territory. Dominant animals are usually the strongest ones.

egg tooth A temporary tooth on the tip of a baby reptile's snout, which the young reptile uses to pierce the shell of its egg. The egg tooth falls off after hatching.

embryo A young reptile developing in an egg or inside its mother's body.

evaporate The process in which water dries up by turning into vapour and escaping into the air.

evolved Changed slowly into a new species over many millions of years.

fang A sharp tooth, often hollow for injecting venom into prey.

flipper A paddle-shaped limb.

forage To actively search for food.

fossil The remains of a long-dead animal or plant preserved as rock. Impressions in rock, such as footprints, can also be fossils.

gland A part of the body that produces special substances for the body to use. Saliva, tears and venom are all produced by glands.

habitat The type of place where an animal naturally lives and to which its body is adapted.

heat-pits Cavities in the head of a snake that can detect the body heat of other animals.

hemipenes The two sex organs of a male snake or lizard. Only one hemipene is used at a time when mating.

hibernate To enter a sleeplike state in which the body functions at a very low level and so uses up little energy. Hibernation helps some animals to survive the winter.

humidity The amount of water vapour in the air.

incubate To keep eggs warm until they are ready to hatch.

intestines A tube inside the body that digests food and absorbs nutrients and water.

Jacobson's organ A pit in the roof of a reptile's mouth that detects airborne scents.

juvenile A young animal that is not yet an adult.

keratin A hard substance from which horns, nails, claws and reptile scales are made.

mammal An animal that has hair (fur) and that feeds its young on milk.

mangroves Coastal forests. Mangrove trees grow in seashore mud, anchored by their long roots. Tides often cover the base of the trees.

mating The coming together of male and female animals to produce young.

migrate To move from place to place in search of food or better weather.

mimicry The way an animal uses colours, patterns and behaviour to make itself resemble another animal.

molluscs A group of animals that includes snails, slugs, octopuses, mussels and squid.

mucus A fluid produced by the body of an animal.

nectar A sugary liquid produced by flowers.

nocturnal Active at night.

organ Part of the body that performs a specific function. The lungs, for example, are organs used for breathing.

osteoderm A lump of bone in a reptile's skin that provides protection against predators. Crocodilians and some lizards have osteoderms.

ovaries The organs in a female animal's body that produce eggs.

paralysing Affecting an animal's nerves or muscles so that it cannot move, but is still alive.

pigments Coloured substances.

predator An animal that hunts other animals for food.

prey The victim of a predator.

rainforest Thick forest in tropical areas where there is heavy rainfall all year round.

reptile A cold-blooded vertebrate with a scaly skin.

ritual display Behaviour that communicates threat, defence or readiness to mate.

rival An animal competing for food, territory or mates.

saliva A colourless liquid produced by glands in the mouth. Saliva moistens food to make it easier to swallow and may also help to digest it.

savanna Large expanses of tropical grassland with a few scattered trees and bushes.

scales Small flat plates that cover the skin and protect it.

scutes Scales that have developed into horny plates.

skeleton A bony framework that supports the body and protects the organs inside it.

skull A hard bony case that protects the brain.

sloughing The way in which snakes and some species of lizards shed their outer layer of skin all at once, rather than gradually, as most animals do.

species A particular type of animal or plant. Members of a species share the same characteristics. They can mate and produce young that are able to breed themselves.

sperm Sex cells produced by a male animal. The sex cells produced by a female are called eggs. In mating, the male's sperm fertilises the female's eggs, so that young can develop inside the egg.

spinal cord A bundle of nerves running down the centre of a vertebrate animal's spine.

spine A long "bone" down the centre of a vertebrate's body, which is actually made up of many smaller bones called vertebrae (singular: vertebra). The spine is also known as the backbone.

stalking Quietly and secretly creeping up on prey.

streamlined Having a sleek shape that allows an animal to move easily through water.

territory An area defended by an animal.

tissue The non-bony parts of an animal's body.

thermoreceptors Cells in a pit viper's heat-pits that can detect temperature changes.

tropical Having a climate that is warm or hot all year round.

undulate To move with an up-and-down motion.

vegetation Plant life.

venom A poisonous liquid used by an animal to kill or paralyse prey. Animals that use poison to kill their prey are said to be venomous.

vertebrate An animal with a spine and an internal skeleton, such as a reptile, mammal, amphibian, fish or bird.

vestigial limbs The stumplike remains of limbs in some snake and lizard species.

voracious Eager to feed.

yolk The yellow part of an egg. The yolk is a store of food that feeds an embryo while it is growing in the egg.

Index

Note: Page numbers in *italic* refer to captions to illustrations. Main references are in **bold**.

A

adders
  puff **92**
  saw-scaled **93**
African pancake tortoise **99**
agamas
  Arabian toad-headed **59**
  common **58**
alligator lizard, southern 72
alligators 29, *29*, *39*
  American *39*, *51–52*, **108**
alligator snapping turtle 27
amphibians 10, 11
anaconda **82**
anole lizard 32, *32*, 33
Arabian toad-headed agama **59**
armadillo lizard **71**
Arrau River turtle **104**

B

banded sea snake **88**
basilisk lizard **51**
basking 17, 38, *38*
Bibron's burrowing asp **83**
big headed turtle **105**
bird predators 47, *47*
birth 9, 37
blind lizard **64**
blind snakes 25, *25*, **79**
blue-tongued skink **49**
boa constrictor **80**
bodies **14–15**
bones **12–13**

boomslang 44, 45, *45*
bowsprit tortoise **97**
brain, lizard 14, *14*
Burton's snake-lizard **65**
bushmaster **95**

C

caiman lizard **67**
caimans 29, *29*, **109**
California legless lizard 22
camouflage and colour **48–49**, *48*, *49*
chameleons *20–21*
  camouflage and colour 48, *48*
  European **60**
  flap-necked **61**
  food and feeding 42, *42*
  Jackson's **60**
  Meller's **61**
chelonians 8, 11, **26–27**
  food/feeding 41, *41*
  hearing 16
  hibernation 39, *39*
  limbs 19, *19*
  organs 15, *15*, 16
  skeleton 12, *12*
chemical weapons 50, *50*
chuckwalla **55**
climbers 19
cobras 44, 46, **90**
collared lizard **56**
colour and camouflage **48–49**
Cook Strait tuatara **54**
coral snakes 49
corn snake *25*
cottonmouth **94**
courtship and mating 18, **32–33**
crocodiles 8, *13*, 28, *28*
  estuarine **111**
  egg-laying 9, 35

food and feeding 41, 43, *43*
  head *29*, *29*
  mugger **110**
  Nile 18, *28*, 35, *35*, 41, *41*, *43*, *43*, **110**
  West African dwarf **111**
  see also crocodilians
crocodilians 8, 11, **28–29**
  ears 16
  food and feeding 40
  heads 14, *14*
  movement 18, 28, *28–29*
  skeleton 12, *12*
  temperature 39
  see also crocodiles

D

defences **50–51**
desert lizards 23, *23*
desert night lizard **71**
De Vis's banded snake **91**
diamondback terrapin **98**
Dibamus Novaeguineae **64**
dinosaurs 10
dragons 9
  flying dragons 23, *23*
  Komodo dragon 22, *22*, **75**
  soa-soa water dragon **59**

E

eagles 47, *47*
earless monitor **75**
ears 16, *16*
eastern box turtle **98**
eastern diamondback 45, *45*, **95**
Eastern green mamba **91**
Echmatemys turtle *10*
egg-eating snake **86**

egg-laying and eggs
34–35, *34*, *35*
amphibians 11
crocodile 9
crocodilians 29, *29*
reptiles 9
Egyptian cobra **90**
elephants 46, *46*
elephant-trunk snake **82**
emerald tree boa **81**
Emoia Cyanogaster **69**
enemies **46–47**
estuarine crocodile **111**
European chameleon **60**
European pond turtle **101**
evolution 10–11, 18
eyes *16*, 17

F

false coral snake **81**
false map turtle **100**
fangs and venom 44, *44*
feet **18–19**
fer-de-lance **92**
Feylinia Cussori **69**
flap-necked chameleon
61
flat lizard, imperial **70**
Florida sand skink **68–69**
folklore 9
food and feeding **40–41**,
40, *41*, 42–43, *42*, *43*
desert lizards 23, *23*
snakes 13, 17
heat detectors 17, *17*
worm lizards 9
fossils 10
frilled lizard *51*

G

Gaboon viper **93**
Galapagos giant tortoise
97
garter snake, common 25,
25, **89**
gavial 29, *29*, **109**

geckos
climbers 19, *19*
Kuhl's **63**
leaf-tailed **64**
leopard **62**
Phelsuma Vinsoni **65**
Sphaerodactylus
parthenopion 22
tokay **62**
web-footed **63**
Gila monster 45, *45*, **73**
gopher tortoise 27, *27*
Gould's monitor **74**
grass snake 50, *50*, **87**
Green sea turtle 26
Green tree boa *30–31*
Great Plains skink **68**

H

habitats 8, 22
hatching 29, *29*
hawksbill **106**
heads 14, *14*, 29, *29*
hearing 16
heat detectors 17, *17*
hibernation 25, 39, *39*
hooded scaly-foot **65**
human predators 26, 47,
47
hunter-killers **42–43**, *42*,
43

I

iguanas 38, **38**
common iguana **55**
forest iguana **57**
marine iguana 40, *40*,
56–57
rhinoceros iguana **57**
imperial flat lizard **70**
incubation 34–35, *34–35*

J

Jackson's chameleon **60**
Jacobson's organ 16

K

killing 42–43, *42*, *43*
king cobra **90**
king snake 49, *49*, **85**
Komodo dragon 22, *22*,
75
Kuhl's gecko **63**

L

leaf-tailed gecko **64**
leatherback **107**
legless lizards 22, *22*
legs **18–19**
leopard gecko **62**
limbs **18–19**, *18*, *19*
lizards 11, 18, 19, **22–23**
brain 14, *14*
camouflage and colour
48, 49
courtship and mating 32,
33, 32–33
defences 50, 51, *51*
ears 16, *16*
egg-laying 34
food 41
Jacobson's organ 16, *16*
scales *13*
species 8
temperature 38
"third eye" 17
venomous 45
young 37
see also worm lizards
loggerhead turtle **107**

M

mamba, eastern green **91**
mangrove snake **89**
white-bellied **84**
mata-mata turtle 43, *43*
mating *see* courtship and
mating
Medusa 9, *9*
Meller's chameleon *61*
Mexican beaded lizard *45*
mimicry 49

mongoose, Indian 46, *46*
monitor lizards 32, *32*
  earless **75**
  Gould's **74**
  Nile **74**
movement 18, 24, 28, 28–29
mugger **110**
Murray River turtle **104**

N

nests **34–35**, *34*, *35*
New Guinea plateless turtle 103, *103*
Nile crocodile *28*, **110**
  egg-laying 35, *35*
  enemies 46
  food and feeding 41, *41*, 43, *43*
  mother and young 36, *36*
  movement *18*
  Nile monitor **74**
  Nile softshell turtle *26*

O

organs **14–15**, *14*, *15*, 33
Oriental fire-bellied toad *11*
osteoderms 13

P

Pacific ridley **106**
paradise tree snake **85**
Phelsuma Vinsoni **65**
plateless turtle, New Guinea **103**
pond slider **101**
predators
  human 26, 47, *47*
  reptiles 42
princely mastigure **58**
puff adder **93**
pythons
  African 42
  Indian **83**

R

rat snake **84**
red-bellied snake **88**
red-blotched shieldtail snake **88**
Rhynchocephalia 54
river terrapin **100**
rubber boa **80**

S

sandfish lizard 38, *38–39*
saw-scaled adder **92**
scales 13, *13*
scaly-foot, hooded **65**
scarlet king snake 49, *49*
Schlegel's blind snake **79**
sea snake, banded **88**
secretary bird 47
senses **16–17**
serrated hingeback tortoise **96**
shells, chelonians 26
sidewinder **94**
sight 16
skeletons **12–13**
skin 13
skinks
  blue-tongued 49, *49*
  climbing 19
  Feylinia Cussori **69**
  Florida sand **68–69**
  Great Plains **68**
  spiny-tailed **67**
sloughing 25, *25*
slow worm **73**
snail-eating snake 40, *40–41*
snake-lizard, Burton's **65**
snakes 8, 11, 18, **24–25**
  birth 37
  camouflage and colour 49, *49*
  constricting 42
  courtship and mating 18, 33, *33*
  defences 50, *50*

egg-laying 34–35, *35*
food and feeding 40, 41, 42, *42*
hearing 16
heat detectors 17, *17*
Jacobson's organ 16, *16*
organs 15, *15*
skeleton 13, *13*
venom 44–45
snapping turtle **105**
soa-soa water dragon **59**
Somali edge snout **77**
sound 16
southern alligator lizard **72**
spectacled caiman **109**
Sphaerodactylus parthenopion 22
spiny softshell turtle **102**
spiny-tailed skink **67**
spotted water snake **86**
spurs 18, *18*
spur-thighed tortoise **99**
starred tortoise *20–21*
stinkpot turtle 50, *50*
strand racerunner **66**
sunbeam snake **79**

T

taipan *33*
tegu, common **66**
temperatures **38–39**
terrapins 11, 96
  diamondback terrapin **98**
  river terrapin **100**
thermoreceptors 17
"third eye" 17
thorny devil 23, *23*
thread snakes 25
timber rattlesnake *17*
toad, Oriental fire-bellied *11*
tokay gecko **62**
tortoises 11, 96
  African pancake **99**
  bowsprit **97**

burrowing 27, *27*
courtship and mating
  33, *33*
food and feeding 41
Galapagos giant **97**
hibernation 39, *39*
limbs 19, *19*
serrated hingeback **96**
spur-thighed **99**
starred *20–21*
  see also chelonians
tree snake **85**
tuataras 8, 17, *17*, **54**
turtles 8, 11, 96
  Arrau River **104**
  big headed **105**
  defences 50, *50*
  eastern box **98**
  Echmatemys 10
  egg-laying 34, *34*
  European pond **101**
  false map **100**
  fresh-water turtles 27
  food 41
  green sea *26*
  hawksbill **106**
  Indian softshell **102**
  leatherback **107**
  limbs 19, *19*
  loggerhead **107**
  marine turtles **26**, 36,
    36–37, 41
  mata-mata 43, **43**
  Murray River **104**
  New Guinea plateless
    103
  Pacific ridley **106**
  pond slider **101**
  snapping turtle **105**
  spiny softshell **102**
  stinkpot 50, *50*
  yellow mud turtle **103**
two-legged worm lizard
  77
two-striped forest pit
  viper *37*

types of reptiles 8
Tyrannosaurus 10, *10*

V

venom **44–45**, *44*, *45*
vertebrates 12
vestigial limbs 18, *18*
vine snake 49, *49*, **87**
vipers 44
  fer-de-lance **92**
  Gaboon viper **93**
  pit vipers 17, *17*, *37*

W

wall lizard **70**
weapons, chemical 50, *50*
web-footed gecko **63**
West African dwarf
  crocodile **111**
Western blind snake **25**
white-bellied mangrove
  snake **84**
white-bellied worm lizard
  76
worm lizards 9, *9*,
  Somali edge snout **77**
  two-legged **77**
  white-bellied **76**

X

Xenosaurus **72**

Y

yellow mud turtle **103**
young
  amphibians 11
  reptiles 9, 36-37, *36*, *37*

International zoos

Here are just a few zoos which house a good variety of reptile species.

AUSTRALIA/NEW ZEALAND
Australian Reptile Park, Somersby, New South Wales
Melbourne Zoo, Parkville, Victoria
Auckland Zoological Park, Western Springs, Auckland

CANADA
Metropolitan Toronto Zoo, Toronto

UNITED KINGDOM
Chester Zoo,
Cheshire, England
Bristol Zoo,
Avon, England
Cotswold Wildlife Park,
Burford, Oxon, England
Edinburgh Zoo,
Murrayfield, Edinburgh, Scotland
Glasgow Zoopark,
Calderpark, Uddingston, Glasgow, Scotland
London Zoo, Regent's Park, London, England
Welsh Mountain Zoo, Colwyn Bay, Clwydd, Wales

UNITED STATES OF AMERICA
Lincoln park Zoo, Chicago, Illinois
Oakland Zoo, Oakland, California
St. Louis Zoo, St. Louis, Missouri

Web sites

Web sites are constantly being expanded or added to. Check out:
REPTILEMANIA!
http://www.gslis.utexas.edu/~lcp/reptile/Repl.html
Kids site with links, fascinating facts and terrible trivia.
CROCODILES
http://www.pbs.org/wgbh/nova/crocs/
All you ever wanted to know about crocodilians, including a "clickable croc" and details on all 23 species.
WORLD OF REPTILES
http://www.natureexplorer.com/WR/WR1.html
In-depth site on these scaly creatures, with sections on each of the main reptile groups.
THE TURTLE PAGES
http://www.crosswinds.net/~theturtlepages.com
Turtle enthusiast's web site.
KID'S QUESTIONS ABOUT TURTLES
http://www.micronet.net/users/~turtle/pondfolder/kidspage/questions
Snappy answers to frequently asked questions and lots of links.
THE BRITISH HERPETOLOGICAL SOCIETY
http://www.thebhs.org
Reptile and amphibian information.

Acknowledgements

ARTISTS

Elizabeth Gray, Steve Kirk, Alan Male, Joannah May, Eric Robson, Simon Turvey, Colin Woolf

PHOTOGRAPHS

l=left; r=right; t=top; b=bottom; c=centre.

4t Marco Modic/Corbis, 4b Premaphotos/BBC Natural History Unit; 5t Lynn Stone/BBC Natural History Unit, 5b Tom Vezo/BBC Natural History Unit; 6-7 Marco Modic/Corbis; 9t Michael Freeman/Corbis, 9b Araldo de Luca/Corbis; 10 Kevin Schafer/Corbis, 13l Bruce Davidson/BBC Natural History Unit, 13r Jonathan Blair/Corbis, 16 Jose B Ruiz/BBC Natural History Unit, 17t Albert Aanensen/BBC Natural History Unit, 17b Joe McDonald/Corbis; 18 John Downer/Oxford Scientific Films; 19 Jal Cooke/Oxford Scientific Films; 20-21 Premaphotos/BBC Natural History Unit; 22 Michael Pitts/BBC Natural History Unit, 25t Zig Leszczynski/Oxford Scientific Films, 25b Nigel Marven/BBC Natural History Unit; 28 Mark Deeble & Victoria Stone/Oxford Scientific Films; 30-31 Lynn Stone/BBC Natural History Unit; 32 A N T/NHPA; 33 & 37 Pete Oxford/BBC Natural History Unit; 39t Lynn Stone/BBC Natural History Unit, 39b Angela Hampton/RSPCA Photo Library; 40 Tui de Roy/Oxford Scientific films; 41t Martha Holmes/BBC Natural History Unit, 41b Bruce Davidson/BBC Natural History Unit; 42 Daryl Balfour/NHPA; 47 Bernard Walton/BBC Natural History Unit; 49 Michael Fogden/Oxford Scientific Films; 50 Philip Sharpe/Oxford Scientific Films; 51 Stephen Dalton/NHPA; 52-53 Tom Vezo/BBC Natural History Unit.

COVER PHOTOGRAPHY/ARTWORK

Front l Eric Robson/Garden Studio, r Powerstock Zefa; back Alan Male.